How To Frame Pictures For Fun And For Profit

By Edward Landon

SUNVILLAGE
publications

www.sunvillagepublications.com

How To Frame Pictures For Fun And Profit
By Edward Landon

Copyright © 2010

Cover photography by Lucian Coman
Cover design by www.WebCopyAlchemy.com

For more titles visit: www.sunvillagepublications.com

CONTENTS

PREFACE

WHILE SOME NEW MATERIALS are available and techniques are somewhat improved, all the various operations of picture framing are still done in basically the same way. Picture framing is still a hand operation and is likely to remain so.

For this reason, the text itself has not been changed because the basic methods involved remain the same. As is well known, fashions in picture frames may change but genuine style is the ideal to strive for. It is difficult to err on the side of simplicity.

The new material incorporated in this edition has been concentrated in Chapter XVI and it is suggested that reference be made to it before beginning any particular operation.

The "Sources of Supplies" has been revised because some of the firms previously listed no longer exist. However, inquiries at the sources mentioned may result in information on where to buy hard-to-get materials.

Publisher's note: It is unlikely that the sources quoted sources are still in existence, but they are provided here to remain true to the original work. Prices are also outdated.

CHAPTER ONE

ABOUT *PICTURE* FRAMES

THE PICTURE FRAME, as it exists today, is derived from the doorway or entrance to temples, palaces and cathedrals. From a functional viewpoint, it might have been more practical to place doors at the sides of these buildings, but the importance of the door framing an impressive picture of the interior was never overlooked.

The need to enhance a picture or bas-relief with a frame is evidenced from the earliest times. The first decorations were necessarily crude; a raised line sometimes being the only ornament.

The earliest examples of frame-like decorations or borders bear a great resemblance to door frames. They were composed of two columns surmounted by a connecting entablature and this form persisted into the 15th century. Even the decorations painted by the artists around the edges of pictures before the introduction of movable frames were similar in form.

As a matter of fact, frames without pictures eventually came into existence because the desire to embellish with Moldings was so strong. Rooms in palaces were arbitrarily paneled with Moldings and their vestigial remains are to be seen today in the senselessly paneled walls of apartments in modern cities.

Movable picture frames for "easel" paintings gained quickly in popularity once they were introduced. Besides the elaborate and intricate wood-carving, ebony, ivory, tortoise shell and mother of pearl were used for inlaid decoration. Gold, silver and every other metal have also been used for frames.

With the perfection of the technique of making large sheets of glass which were in turn used to cover and protect pictures, frame-making received a big impetus in the 17th century. In the 18th century, when cheaper mirrors were introduced, frames were in greater demand than ever.

This century also saw an invention that was to revolutionize the art of frame decoration—that of the development of molded composition ornaments. The use of this easily handled material, which did away with the need for laborious and expensive hand-carving, drove artisans to other fields. Since then, there has been no large group of wood-carvers devoted solely to frame decoration.

It is interesting to note that during the Renaissance period, when movable frames were first introduced, book decoration reached its highest form. Undoubtedly, the early carvers and framers, besides using architectural designs, took many of their ideas from early illuminated manuscripts. The frames of the Louis' periods certainly got their inspiration from typographical decorative motifs. Before then, architects and sculptors designed much of the scroll-work, but later goldsmiths were employed for decoration. Over-elaboration became the order of the day until all forms were lost beneath the gingerbread.

With the French revolution, people turned away from all evidences of bourgeois wealth and returned to a refreshing simplicity. Until 1850 all Moldings were cut from rough boards by hand, but with the invention of laborsaving machinery, frames could be put on the market for what the raw material had cost previously. This country was fortunately spared from the use of molded ornaments until the advent of the Victorian era. American frames up to that time were relatively simple and dignified, very often using only natural, stained wood and a gilded insert The carving, when used, was restricted to the classical forms of ornamentation for specific molding shapes.

The frame-makers who constructed the monstrosities of the Victorian era were not content to put one heavily embellished gold frame around a picture of "The Stag at Bay" or something similar, but three or four. This birthday cake was then enclosed in a glass-covered, plush-lined, mahogany shadow-box. This was presumably for protection, but its need is a mystery since the interiors of that time were heavily shaded and hermetically sealed anyway.

AD INFINITUM!

Around 1900 there was a fashion for "Oxford", plush and cork-decorated frames. Hours and hours were spent carving these horrors and fitting them intricately together or in decorating frames with segments of cork. They can be found only rarely today, even in the higher priced second-hand stores, euphemistically called "antique shops". But perhaps it is too early to drag out another "antique" vogue. Mass production, to some degree at least, has forced a healthy simplification.

At the same time that heavy gilt frames were the vogue for oil paintings, a demand for polished, veneered oak and white enamel frames developed. In order to cheapen the cost of production, a fashion was instituted for bronze frames, i.e., frames finished with gold or silver paint. It did not last long, however, and simple, wide frames in black or dark brown wood of the Flemish type came into favor.

"An *inexpensive picture* frame *may be made by* covering a *plain pine frame with varnish, then sprinkling it lavishly with either sand, oatmeal or rice. When thoroughly dry, cover the whole surface with gold paint"—From a ladies magazine of* 1894.

As will be seen from this quotation, one of the causes of a great deal of misconception regarding proper framing is the damage which has been done by the "ideas" put forth in women's magazines and slick-paper decorators' journals. The attempts at being "cute" and "homey" in the women's magazines and the chi-chi attitude of being "smart" in the more expensive journals are on a par for bad taste. There is no reason to suppose that any of the suggestions they make today are any improvement basically over those advanced fifty years ago.

Just as all decorative art continued in the doldrums until the influence of the "modern" art of the Paris Exposition of 1925 was felt, so picture framing had its minor ups and downs in design.

In the late twenties there was a less hide-bound attitude toward picture frames and color, in place of gilt or gloomy black, began to appear. Picture framing has lagged, to some extent, behind the advances made in the best of contemporary furniture design for example, but that is to be expected since the bulk of

4

home furnishings produced in this country is in execrable taste.

While the major part of the framing being done today is still in poor taste, one can avoid contributing to it by following a simple guide for good, conventional work. Always consider the finish of the frame first in relation to the picture and only later to the colors of draperies, furniture or walls. The result will be that if the picture itself is really suited to the room, the frame will also be harmonious. Of course, there are no hard and fast rules in framing, and at times a slight variation in hue or value will certainly not hurt the picture but may make it more in keeping with the interior for which it is destined.

Three qualities are essential for good picture framing; taste, proportion and craftsmanship in that order. In framing, it is difficult to err on the side of simplicity. Advantage should be taken of good tradition, but the needs of modern living must be kept in mind. The artist and craftsman should not be swayed by "fads'* in framing such as covering a Victorian atrocity with whitewash and calling it "smart". The three requisites mentioned above can only be developed with time and through experience. However, if sufficient study is given to the picture before it is framed, errors will be reduced and better frames will result.

Before either making or finishing the frame it should be remembered that the proportions, that is, the width and depth or "profile" of the molding is of more importance than the finish. It is much easier to commit the fault of "over-framing" a picture than it is to make the frame too plain or narrow.

5

The following general rule should always be borne in mind: The more elaborate, colorful or detailed the picture, the simpler should be the frame and vice versa.

A monotonous effect can be avoided easily by giving the frame an interesting textural finish or by decorating it with a continuous line of geometrical shapes. These should be based on the seven primary forms so well outlined in the book A Method for *Creative Design* by Adolfo Best-Maugard. Applied singly or in combination, along the outside, the inside, on the face or a raised portion of the molding, the decoration will be unobtrusive and yet provide interest. The combinations of carving, texture and color are almost endless, therefore no picture need be without its individual, perfect finish.

There is a good tendency today towards minimizing the heavy ornamentation of so-called antique or Barbizon-type frames by giving them an all-over neutral effect with only touches of color or gilt as accents.

The beginner in frame-making is often confused as to the choice of molding or finish for a particular picture and therefore falls back on the practice of copying a frame or finish he has seen elsewhere. Everyone learns by imitation, but it is certainly better to develop one's own critical faculties by trying to work out each problem individually. Since framing *is* a skill that requires experience to develop to the point of real facility, analysis of each framing problem by oneself will add to confidence and the next job will be that much easier to do.

Picture framing follows all general changes in sound decorative style, so no one can expect to produce a frame which need never be changed. By keeping the principles of good taste always in mind, we will not turn out something faddish or freakish. There will be times when a small or even tiny picture gains in importance and is not necessarily over-powered by a very wide molding if used judiciously. Again, a very large picture may only require the simplest of narrow Moldings to set it off properly. There is no call to be precious, but care employed when choosing the exact value of color for the frame or mat may make a tremendous difference in the final effect.

A few words on present-day, conventional picture framing might be in order—but just a few. Extended discussion of contemporary methods of framing would be wasted; styles and fashions in frames will undoubtedly change in a relatively short time. Therefore, the following are only general indications of how pictures in various mediums are ordinarily framed at the present time.

Original prints in black and white such as etchings, lithographs, etc., are usually matted in white, off-white or cream mats and framed with glass in very narrow Moldings of natural wood or black. A narrow gold line is sometimes added to relieve the severity of the black frame.

Original color prints, as distinguished from reproductions, such as color wood-blocks, colored etchings or lithographs and serigraphs are also matted and then framed in narrow Moldings with glass. More latitude in the use of color in both mats and frames for

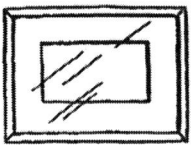

WATER COLOR

this type of picture is becoming increasingly popular.

Water-colors are usually put in proportionately larger mats and the frames are somewhat wider. Glass is always used with water-colors. Frames for them are still being made in simple, natural wood or painted finishes, but with the tendency to give the medium the importance it deserves, they are often as heavy, decorated and textured as are those for oil paintings.

The frames for pastels are similar to the ones used for water-colors, except that they are matted only when necessary. Class is always used, as is a concealed insert to separate the picture from contact with the glass surface.

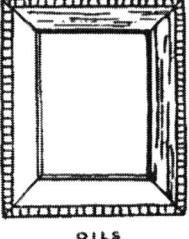

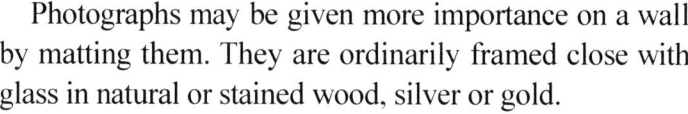

OILS

Oil paintings are framed closely except for the occasional use of extra-wide inserts, which give the appearance of mats. It has been popular lately to employ less ornamentation and gilding and to bring the finish into closer relationship with the picture.

Photographs may be given more importance on a wall by matting them. They are ordinarily framed close with glass in natural or stained wood, silver or gold.

Fine reproductions of oil paintings, water-colors and prints are framed to resemble their originals.

No other decoration in a room is of such importance as a picture. Correctly framed, it can furnish continual esthetic enjoyment; badly framed, it will merely be a jarring disturbance. Perhaps the artist should take a hint from good salesmanship; present your product in the most attractive manner possible. The right frame can improve the appearance of any picture.

CHAPTER TWO

TOOLS AND *EQUIPMENT*

WHILE GOOD TASTE is to be observed in all the stages of picture framing, good craftsmanship is the first requirement when working with tools and actually making the frame. Time spent in sound construction will not only reduce the necessity for repairs, but will help develop the beginner's skill and speed. It takes but a few minutes longer to make a strong joint than it does a poor one.

Because the joint used in picture frame-making is the weakest in all woodworking (end grain to end grain), it is necessary to make every effort to strengthen it. Nails or screws alone are not enough; the joint must be properly glued with either hot cabinet glue, casein glue or, best of all, the new plastic resin glue now on the market. The last named is mixed with cold water in the exact amount needed so that there is no waste, and as it dries harder and harder becomes waterproof and is not affected by climatic changes of humidity or temperature. Brushes used for glue are best made from artists' oil-painting bristle brushes by cutting down the handles to five or six inches in length.

It is necessary to use tools of good quality in order to make sound joints. Cheap tools will not do the work efficiently and are constantly in need of replacement. If it is seriously planned to make frames regularly, the investment in quality tools will not only facilitate the work but will be less expensive in the long run. A full range of cabinet maker's tools is not necessary, but as more experience is gained, the framer will find a need for items other than the ones described in the following.

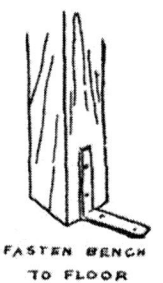

FASTEN BENCH
TO FLOOR

The first piece of equipment needed for good work is the BENCH. It should be large enough to handle any frame contemplated and high enough (32" to 36") for comfortable work. Keep it away from the wall so that it can be reached from all sides when working on large frames and fasten it to the floor if possible for added strength.

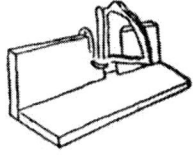

The MITER BOX is used for cutting the miters for the corners of frames. It can be of the home-made variety costing a few cents or it can be purchased for about 50c for the wooden kind to the metal box costing as much as $20.00. Because accuracy is absolutely essential when cutting miters, it is not advisable to try to use a home-made affair or to buy a miter box costing less than $4.00 to $5.00. Any hardware dealer will be glad to show his stock and a box can be selected easily that will fill one's needs and which is sturdy and accurate enough not to need replacement.

The BACK-SAW should be of the best quality in order to retain its set and sharpness. Inferior saws need constant re-setting and sharpening and unless it can be done at home, it will soon be found that much more has been spent on conditioning than the saw originally cost. Almost any length can be used, but a 20" long, 4" wide saw with at least 12 teeth to the inch will be most adequate. Handle the saw with care, do not cut into nails or screws, and keep it hung up when not in use.

For making frames with any degree of professional accuracy and finish in joining, a MITER VISE or CRAMPING TOOL is essential. Like the miter box, this can also be home-made or an efficient, ready-made kind can be purchased. It is used to hold the corners firmly together while joining. If one has ever tried making frames without it, further argument for their necessity is superfluous. A small vise, capable of joining Moldings up to 4" wide has been on the market for many years. For those who do not wish to invest in one at the start, there are other methods of joining such as by the use of clamps alone, a homemade jig or cramping tool. They are all described at the end of this section. However, none of the substitutes for a regular picture framing miter vise will do the work of holding the corners together as efficiently as the ready-made tool designed for that purpose. The time spent in making a home-made affair, together with the difficulty of producing first class work with it, will be wasted unless the beginner only intends making frames very rarely.

The COMBINATION MITER BOX, SAW AND MITER VISE eliminates the individual purchase or construction of the three tools already discussed and combines them into one. The most popular one on the market handles Moldings up to 4½" in width by about 4" deep. It will join any frame larger than 7½" x 7½". The back saw furnished with the machine is carefully fitted and can be adjusted easily for depth of cut. The machine is compact and

11

can be attached readily to one corner of a workbench. The investment is not high, and if the total cost of any of the first three tools and their inefficient operation is considered, it will be seen that its purchase should be seriously contemplated by the beginner in frame-making.

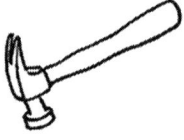

Care should be used in the selection of the HAMMER, not only for price and quality but for the balance or "feel". A badly balanced or too heavy a hammer will tire the wrist very quickly and thus contribute to poor work. Buy a "claw" nail hammer of some well-known brand. Ask to see hammers weighing from 13 to 20 ounces and choose the one that feels right. As one progresses in framing, other hammers will be found useful, but one is enough to begin with.

The NAIL-SET is used for driving nails below the surface of the wood so that the holes can be filled and the surface smoothed. Purchase a good quality, square head 1/16" nail set. Other sizes may be needed later on.

PLIERS are useful for pulling nails which may have been wrongly started as well as other odd jobs. Buy a medium size, side-cutting pair of good quality.

The HAND DRILL is essential for drilling holes before driving nails or screws when joining the frame. The cheaper varieties work fairly well but good quality hand drills have strong gripping jaws, easier action and will last longer. When buying, see that the gears mesh and turn smoothly and that there is a minimum of "play". Buy the length that seems best, but the smaller sizes are just as adequate for frame-making.

A set of DRILLS is also necessary. There will be a

certain amount of bending and breakage when using these, but the cost is comparatively low. A set of them should be acquired which will be large enough in variety of size so that the right one will be available for the nail or screw being used. Specific sizes are difficult to recommend, but after a few frames have been made, it will be easy to see which ones are most needed. It is suggested that one buys twist drills in sizes 25, 33, 44, 50, 55 and 58 to begin with. They will be sufficient for the use of small, medium and large size nails. Buy the drills at the same time that brads and nails are purchased, matching them in size as closely as possible.

Since screws are used ordinarily only with heavy molding, a medium to heavy SCREW-DRIVER will be needed. One with a 6" to 10" blade will be of most use.

A PLANE will be found useful in giving a different shape to Moldings as well as for smoothing and other work. A steel JACK-PLANE, 11½" long or longer is a valuable addition to the tool list.

A set of small WOOD FILES or RASPS will be needed for the decoration of plain Moldings and will also be found useful for general shaping or the smoothing of ornaments. 8" long rasps are ample. Buy one of each. Round, flat, triangular and half-round with handles for them.

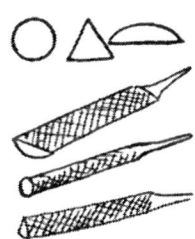

Even if it is not planned to cut glass for the first frames one makes, a GLASS-CUTTER will be handy to have for the future. Its low cost makes it a necessity.

The more CLAMPS owned, the better. One can begin by buying two or four wooden joiner's

clamps and as many small C-CLAMPS as possible.

A TRY-SQUARE will be needed to check on the square ness of the comers of frames while joining. An 8" try-square with a wooden handle is recommended rather than a larger, flat, steel square because it can fit inside smaller frames and still be long enough to insure accuracy. The wooden-handled type is also cheaper.

The COUNTERSINK is a bit for the hand drill and is used to make a shallow, tapering hole to sink the head of a screw below the surface of the wood. Be sure to buy one that has a shank small enough to fit the hand drill.

Thus far, only the tools essential for frame-making and joining have been discussed. A few more items are needed if the framer intends to cut mats, mount pictures and do his own assembling.

There are many knives sold especially for mat-cutting and many other types are suitable for the purpose. Since one should be selected that works best for the individual, only a few general rules for its purchase can be given. The blade of the MAT-KNIFE should be quite short and thin. It should be of high quality steel, capable of being sharpened to a razor edge and of holding it for a while. Paper will dull a cutting edge quicker than any other material, therefore constant re-sharpening is necessary. Because of this fact, the blade should either be of the adjustable variety (sliding into and through the handle) or the blades should be of the type that are easily replaced after being worn down through sharpening.

The STRAIGHT EDGE should be a metal-edged,

14

beveled ruler or, better still, an all-metal straight edge. The extra weight and long-wearing, accurate qualities of the latter sort should compensate for the increased cost. At any rate, sight along the edge or otherwise test it for freedom from warping before buying.

Mats or any other kind of board cannot be cut properly or successfully without constant sharpening of the knife. It is advisable to buy a two-sided SHARPENING STONE, that is, one side medium coarse and the other fine grain. A 6" or 8" stone will be adequate. Use plenty of light machine oil when sharpening.

It is necessary to purchase an accurate RULER or scale. Mistakes will be considerably lessened through its use. Do not attempt to economize on this item because correct measurements are indispensable in frame-making. Buy either a good quality, straight yardstick, a six-foot steel tape rule of the semi-rigid type or a six-foot folding carpenter's rule.

Regular CABINET GLUE may be used with good results for joining although the new synthetic resin glue is preferable. Hot cabinet glue has other uses, however, such as gluing cloth to wood for inserts, backing, attaching mats to mounted pictures, etc.

For the efficient melting of cabinet glue, a GLUE-POT is essential. The beginner in frame-making can perhaps do without one until its need is felt. Two tin cans, one smaller than the other, can be used to make a temporary double boiler.

A few CHISELS will always be of use to the frame-maker. Do not buy them with too short a blade. While they are not absolutely essential, need for them

15

will be soon apparent. Chisels ¼, ½ and 1" wide are adequate.

Good mounting work cannot be done without a heavy ROLLER. Air bubbles are easily removed and good adherence of the mounted picture assured with its use. In this case, a home-made roller constructed from a worn-out washing machine roller or an old rolling pin cut down in length, covered with felt and fitted with a strong handle will serve as well as a ready-made hand roller for laying linoleum. However, sufficient pressure must be exerted while rolling to make up for the loss in weight. A piece of heavy band iron should be bent to fit each end and to form a good-sized handle in the center.

A package of glass PUSH-PINS in the larger size will be found easier to handle than thumb-tacks and will thus speed up the work of mounting. They are used to hold down the corners of pictures and prevent curling while moistening or applying adhesive.

A bone PAPER FOLDER is not indispensable, but a useful implement to iron out stubborn wrinkles when mounting. The smooth handle of a knife or something similar might serve as well.

BATTENS are home-made, felt-covered, wooden strips used as pads when assembling pictures to prevent marring the face of finished frames. A full description of how they can be made is included in the section on assembling.

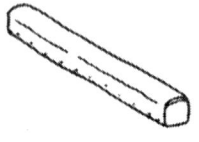

A FLAT-SIDED HAMMER is used for fastening pictures in their frames. It may be either a small, light-weight tack hammer with one side ground flat or a flat-sided TINNER'S SETTING or PANEING

HAMMER of eight or twelve ounces. The light weight is essential so that the blows struck to drive the brads in will not be so heavy as to loosen the corners of the frame. The flat side is necessary because otherwise it would be impossible to strike the head of the brad as it is being driven into the frame.

The FITTING TOOL is an extremely useful implement made especially for fastening pictures in their frames. It is practically essential when driving brads into narrow Moldings. Because it can be adjusted to drive the brads to an exact depth, the danger of forcing them completely through the molding is eliminated. It has a deep throat for wider Moldings and will speed up assembling considerably. Assembling can be done without it, but its purchase is recommended to those craftsmen making frames regularly.

A small CABINET SCRAPER will always be of use for general work in frame-making but especially for cleaning out the rabbet before assembling. The 5 and 10c stores have suitable scrapers.

POWER TOOLS

The following is addressed to those who wish to make picture frames for others as a source of added income or as a full-time occupation.

Heretofore, only the simplest of rudimentary equipment for frame-making has been considered. The subject of motor-driven power tools is one which will be familiar to the home wood-working craftsman, but to the beginner is usually unknown. The following is a rough explanation of their use and how they can be adapted to picture framing.

17

It is assumed that by the time the framer is ready to acquire any power tools, he will already own the basic equipment for doing all the operations in picture framing by hand. The proper combination saw and miter vise will be owned, together with a good range of hand tools including planes, hammers, etc. The purchase of the following equipment is not recommended unless frames are to be made regularly and in quantity.

The most useful power driven tool for picture framing work is the CIRCULAR or BENCH SAW. With the proper attachments, this tool can be made to turn out almost any profile of molding desired besides cutting miters, handling odd jobs and speeding up work tremendously. Inserts of exact width and shape for special jobs can be rapidly executed as can the innumerable strips of varying thickness which are so often used in framing. It can be utilized for cutting strips of decorative molding, etc., thus eliminating the laborious work of hand-filing or carving. Because its use and operation belongs primarily to wood-working generally and not picture framing in particular, further explanation here is unnecessary; the subject is completely covered in handbooks.

The bench saw, then, should be the first power tool whose purchase is to be considered by the serious picture framer. As with all tools, money is thrown away unless quality is the first criterion in selection. Only acquire the type of bench saw which is capable of numerous adjustments and with which the proper attachments, such as molding cutters, can be used. The motor, which is bought separately, should always be of sufficient horse-power to utilize the saw to its fullest capacity. If the motor is too light, it will only stall when in use. For instance, an 8" saw needs a ½ HP motor.

A combination BELT and DISC SANDER is another power tool which will be found of great use in the making of picture frames. It can be employed to smooth molding, thus cutting down a great deal of the hand-sanding usually necessary. Nail holes which have been filled can be smoothed in a matter of seconds. The disc can be employed as a shooting board, insuring good gluing surfaces with a minimum of effort. Other uses will suggest themselves, and it only remains to recommend that this be the next power tool purchased. Belt sanders are not very expensive and only require a ¼ HP motor for operation.

The above tools, together with a complete assortment of hand tools, will be found adequate for the solution of almost any problem which the framer is likely to encounter.

Other power tools, which would be handy to have but which are more or less luxuries include the COPING or JIG SAW and the DRILL PRESS or an electric HAND DRILL. Literature on their uses is plentiful.

Besides the power tools described, several types of automatic hand miter machines are also on the market. Called "choppers" by the trade, they are used by large commercial manufacturers of picture frames. With their use, the miters for 75 or more frames can be cut in an hour.

19

BRADS, NAILS AND SCREWS

While the home craftsman or anyone who has done woodworking to any extent is familiar with brads, nails, screws and dowels, information for the beginner may be useful. Picture framing, unlike other woodworking, is so specialized that in order to achieve the best results, it is very important to choose the right type and size of fastener for each job.

None of the above fasteners are expensive and so it is better when starting out to make frames to buy a wide variety of sizes and lengths in small quantities. After it has been discovered which nails and brads are most commonly used, they can be purchased in larger amounts. Other sizes should be kept on hand, however, for unexpected needs.

If the majority of frames to be made are for prints or water-colors, etc., it will be necessary to have thinner nails and brads for the narrower Moldings used. For Moldings designed for oil paintings, nails up to 3" may be necessary. Because screws are usually only employed for joining extra large Moldings, they should not be in short lengths and should not be too heavy in any case.

BRADS are packed in small boxes labeled with their length and number which indicates the size of wire from which they were made. The numbers are low for heavy, thick brads and high for fine, thin ones. Not all lengths are made in all numbers; usually the shorter lengths are only made in the higher numbers and vice versa. It will be found more practical to avoid the very lowest numbers except in lengths over ⅞".

As a suggestion, brads might be purchased as follows: ⅜" or ½" by 20, ⅝" by 20, ¾" or ⅞" by 18 and 1" by 17.

The NAILS used for joining picture frames are called "finishing" nails. They have a small, rounded head and not a large flat one as do common nails. The head is made in that way so that it may readily be driven or "set" below the surface. Finishing nails are sold from 1" to 4" long (advancing by ¼'s) and their weight depends on their length. It is comparatively easy to find the correct size of nail for a particular frame by laying it across a mitered corner which has been placed together. The nail should be long enough to exceed through one piece and about the same distance into the other, although this is not always possible, on the wider Moldings. If the molding is too wide or of such shape that even nails or screws are not adequate, use what is possible near the corner and provide additional reinforcement by some other method near the inside.

SCREWS are also sold by length and number in the same way that are brads. It is not advisable to buy many screws until it is seen whether they will be needed. Screws shorter than 1½" will be used rarely and only for special work. When drilling holes for screws, always have that part of the corner through which it is to pass first drilled with a hole large enough to permit the screws to slide through. The hole should be continued into the other part with a drill only as large as the "shank" of the screw.

DOWELS are perfectly round pieces of wood sold in varying lengths and in sizes from ⅛" to 1", the

21

usual length being 36". A few of them in different sizes will be found useful to have on hand.

In any event, go slow about stocking up. It may be discovered that a particular method of joining is preferred or that one tends to make up only a certain type of frame.

1. MITER VISE (Home-Made)

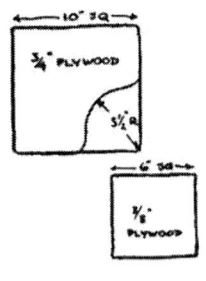

Two screw-type window locks are required for this vise together with two pieces of wood cut to the size and shape shown. By making two of these vises, Moldings in a large variety of widths may be joined.

First, take a piece of ¾" plywood 10" square and cut away the curved area shown. Second, cut a piece of ⅜ plywood 6" square and attach it with screws to the larger piece. Make absolutely sure that the corner nearest the curved part is a perfect right angle, or the joints made with it will not be true. Now attach the window locks in the position shown. They should be at exactly 90^0 to the sides of the top piece.

Its operation will be readily apparent. Each of the screw clamps holds one of the parts of the frame to be joined while fastening. When using the vise, always be sure to place slips of wood between the head of the screw and the molding to avoid damaging the edges.

This vise should not be used for joining the larger, heavier types of molding unless screws alone are used for fastening. The clamps are not strong enough to hold the molding firmly under the blows of the hammer.

2. WEDGE CRAMP *(Home-Made)*

This is a simple type of cramp for holding the corners together while joining. All that is needed is a piece of 1 x 3 x 12 pine for the base. Two pieces (A-A) measuring 1 x 2 x 5 are attached with screws as shown. A triangular piece with 50^0 angles is then fastened in the exact center. Two wedges, made of hardwood, ⅜" thick and about 9" long, tapering from ½" to 3" at the broad ends.

First smooth the base carefully and make sure that it is absolutely flat. Then make the two pieces of 1 x 2 stock about 5" long and attach them at exactly 45^0 to the base so that they form a perfect right angle but with the corner open about 5" as shown. Next cut the triangular piece with the 50^0 angles and screw it accurately in the center. The wedges are then made of ⅜" hardwood running from ½ at one end to 3" at the other. Notches should be cut in them for knocking out after the corner has been joined. Now saw off the projecting corners and sand smooth.

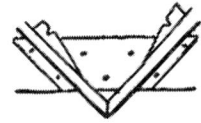

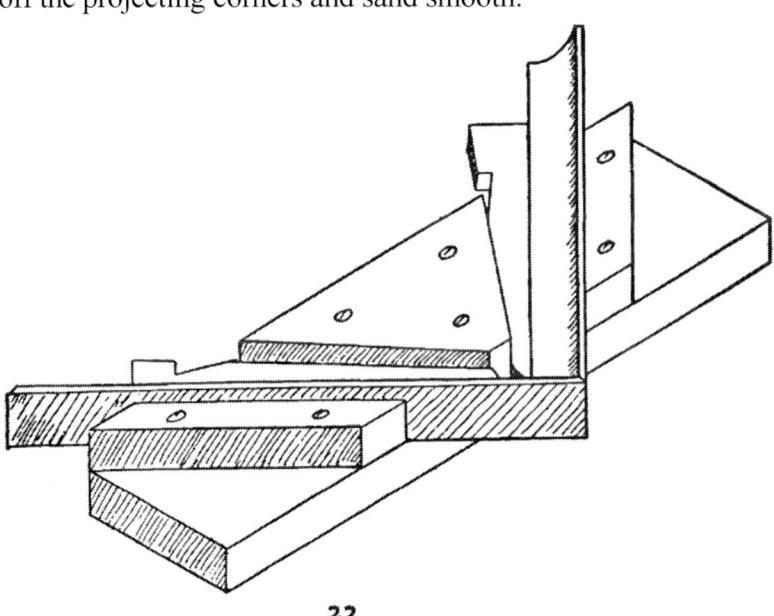

23

When using the cramp it should be fastened securely to the bench so that the corner of the frame being joined is in line with the corner of the bench. The frame will then project over the bench and can be supported in a level position while fastening.

When nailing the miter, it is advisable to clamp the molding down as an added precaution to prevent shifting.

3. WEDGE CRAMP (Home-Made)

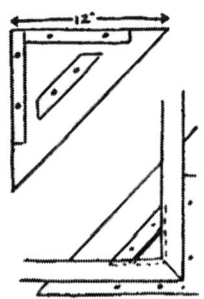

Another type of cramp can be made which, though it does not have the flexibility of the previous one for holding Moldings of varying widths, will work well if molding of approximately the same size is used regularly. Several cramps of this type might be made to accommodate different widths.

Cut a triangular piece of ¾" plywood from a square measuring about 12" by 12". Screw two pieces of hardwood ¼ x 1" x 8" or 10" on the corner to form a perfect right angle as shown.

Next cut a right triangle of the same 1/4" hardwood stock as shown. Place a corner of the molding to be joined on the cramp, slip the triangle in place and then attach a piece ¼ x 1" x 6" as illustrated, leaving space to hammer in a few thin wedges.

If a number of frames of the same size are to be made regularly, four cramps of this kind, one for each corner, should be attached to a piece of plywood of the correct size. In this way the frame can be assembled, glued and joined without shifting until it is completely fastened.

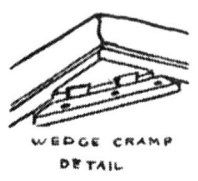

WEDGE CRAMP
DETAIL

When using this cramp, be sure to place small

24

squares of paper under each corner being joined to prevent the frame from sticking to the board or base. As before, it is advisable to clamp the molding with wood-clamps while nailing.

4. ROPE CRAMP (Home-Made)

Another sort of cramp involves the use of four corner blocks and a strong cord. The only disadvantage of this device is that the corners cannot be nailed until the glue has dried and the blocks removed. Strong clamping pressure can be exerted, however, so that a tightly glued joint is made.

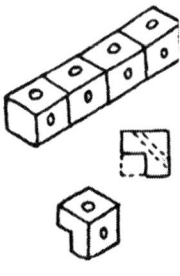

Take a 1" x 1" square piece of hardwood, 4" long and drill four ¼" holes at a 45^0 angle as illustrated. Saw the four pieces apart into 1" lengths and then cut a ½" x ½" section out of each corner opposite the drilled edge. Sandpaper smooth, particularly the holes, so that the cord will not be worn excessively.

The cord used for the cramp must be of the hard, woven, non-stretching variety such as that used for Venetian blinds. It can be purchased in any length at window shade stores.

When using the cramp, allow plenty of slack and take up the difference by twisting with a piece of doweling sufficiently long so that it can be snapped under the frame while the glue is drying.

Another method of making the corner blocks so that the frame can be nailed while the glue is drying is to use four pieces of band-iron bent to almost a right angle and cut and drilled as shown. Unless metal working tools are owned, it is better to have a small machine shop make these up to specifications. When

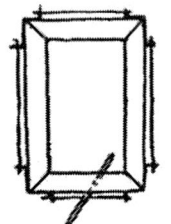

using this type of corner block, three pieces of the cord are to be knotted at the correct places with the knots outside to make a loose fit. Leave one side with plenty of slack to take up the twisting necessary for tightening. While the cords can be shortened or lengthened easily, it will be seen that this type of cramp is limited in use.

5. WIRE CLAMPS FOR CRAMPING

Simple clamps for holding the corners together while the glue is drying and for later nailing can be made easily from upholstery springs. Cut off a section as shown and sharpen the ends by filing or grinding. Lay the corner to be joined together on a flat surface and pull the clamp apart until it can be placed in position, then release carefully. As many as necessary should be attached in different positions to each corner.

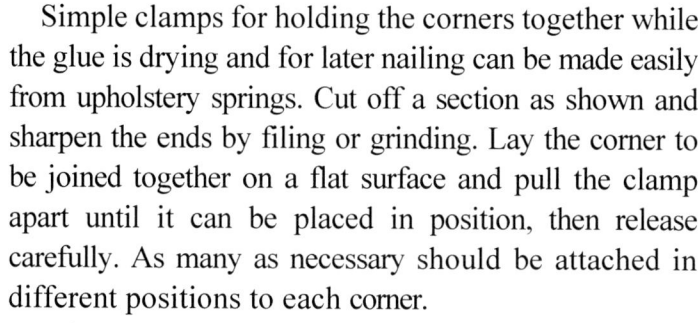

CUT INTO SECTIONS

SECTION

BEND TO SHAPE
AND SHARPEN ENDS

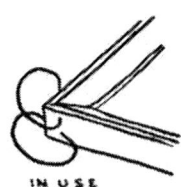

IN USE

Other vises or cramps will most likely occur to the beginner if he is working with home-made equipment, but none of them will give the quick, precise results accomplished with the ready-made tool specifically designed for the purpose.

ESSENTIAL TOOLS FOR CUTTING AND JOINING FRAMES:
    Miter Box
    Back Saw
    Miter Vise or Cramping Tool or Combination Saw,
        Miter Box and Miter Vise
    Screwdriver
    Hammer
    Pliers

26

Hand Drill
Set of Drills
Set of Rasps
Ruler
Nail Set
Try Square
Countersink Bit (Round Shank)
Clamps
Brads, Finishing Nails, Screws
Glue ADDITIONAL TOOLS TO BE NEEDED
LATER:
Glue Pot
Chisels
Jack Plane

TOOLS ESSENTIAL FOR THE OPERATIONS LISTED:
Mat-Cutting:
Mat Knife
Oil Stone
Straight Edge

Mounting: Roller
Push-Pins Bone Paper
Folder Brushes

Assembling:
Battens (Home-Made) Flat
Sided Hammer Fitting
Tool Cabinet Scraper
Glass-Cutter

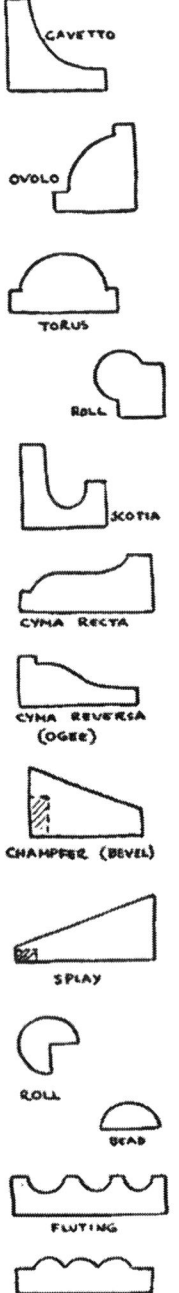

CHAPTER THREE

MOLDINGS

A MOLDING IS A BREAK in a flat surface designed to form an accent by catching light and shade. The various basic shapes of Moldings and their technical names are shown herewith. All Moldings, however, can be classified broadly into three categories: Flat or angular, single-curved and compound. The last named may be a combination of two different curves or of curves and angles together. These combinations make possible very involved and complex molding designs.

Certain ornaments form the decoration traditionally applied to the different types. The classical use of embellishment is as follows: Egg and dart is used for the ovolo, wreath forms for the torus, bead (beading) and real (rope) for the astragal, anthemion and acanthus for the cyma recta and water-leaf for the cyma reversa.

Moldings in general are always designated by their "profile". A deep profile would be a molding having a high outside edge like the splay and a high profile would be similar to the champfer. Wide, narrow and shallow profiles are self-explanatory.

The profile of a molding is the cross-section or end-view and many beginners find it extremely difficult to visualize a molding or a finished frame from this view only. It is therefore important to form a

28

mental picture of the type of frame one has in mind and then to try drawing a cross-section of the molding for practice. Unless this is done (even if the molding is selected directly from stock), one will be frequently disappointed when the frame is made.

It is often necessary, when selecting ready-made frames for finishing from a catalogue, to choose them by the profile alone. They may appear precisely the opposite of what was expected unless extension of their finished appearance can be made mentally.

To make the foregoing clearer, the view of the molding shown herewith is called the profile. Its various parts have been lettered for identification.

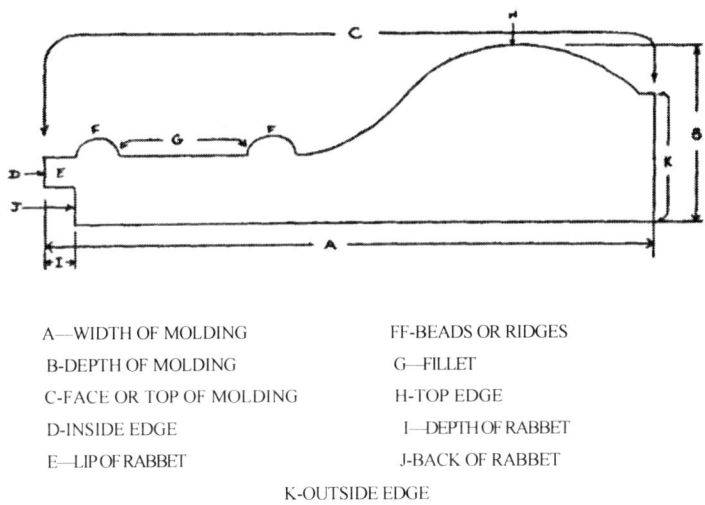

A—WIDTH OF MOLDING	FF-BEADS OR RIDGES
B-DEPTH OF MOLDING	G—FILLET
C-FACE OR TOP OF MOLDING	H-TOP EDGE
D-INSIDE EDGE	I—DEPTH OF RABBET
E—LIP OF RABBET	J-BACK OF RABBET
	K-OUTSIDE EDGE

Throughout this book references will be made to the different sections of a frame and if in doubt as to what part of the frame is meant in a description, reference to the diagram will clarify the point. Throughout the text, effort has been made to explain other framing terms which may seem confusing to the non-professional. The serious beginner will do well to familiarize himself with the technical terms used in the picture framing trade.

Assuming that most artists or home craftsmen do not possess sufficient power tools to turn out all the styles of Moldings which may be needed for different pictures, it will be necessary first to discuss the use of ready-made Moldings and their substitutes.

Unless it is planned to make frames only very rarely, it will be found much more satisfactory to buy ready-made Moldings from a company specializing in them. They will be uniform in quality and size, and professional frames can be produced much more rapidly from them. Besides, a large quantity will not have to be ordered as would be the case if a molding was designed and specially turned out at a lumber mill.

Naturally, special needs are to be the first consideration, but unless some experience has been had in frame making, it is wiser to select the plainer types in the beginning. The basic molding for oil paintings or other large pictures should have character but should also be quite simple in profile. It should be wide enough to be useful for experimentation with bold, severe decoration. Its plainness will permit the addition of strips of other decorative Moldings such as rope or beading to give it interest and variety.

As a suggestion, a 2½" to 3" wide, ordinary scoop molding might be chosen as the first basic shape. The inside or top edge can be decorated with a simple geometric design. Beading, etc., can be easily applied

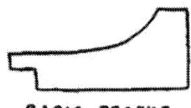

BASIC PROFILE

30

and textured finishes will show up well. Enough should be purchased for several frames at first, and plans made to make each one as different in decoration and finish as possible.

For smaller pictures, water-colors and pictures with glass and mats, a narrower stock molding should be selected. This molding, perhaps 1½′ wide, could be a little more involved in profile since it would not necessarily need the curved decorations. Textured and painted finishes should certainly give enough variety.

Lastly, it will be wise to have on hand varying widths of flat, plain Moldings which can be used for prints or drawings or as inserts for larger pictures. Inserts are frames inside of frames and are of great value for reducing the size of large frames. They will be dealt with in detail in a separate section.

In all of these Moldings, the beginner should attempt to secure basswood, whitewood or white pine. These close-grained, easily worked woods reduce the danger of splitting and are readily carved. Oak, birch, maple, etc., while attractive for their natural grains, should be left until one has gained enough wood-working experience.

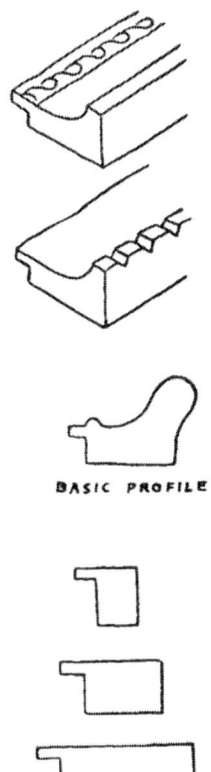

BASIC PROFILE

LUMBER YARD BUILDER'S MOLDINGS

If, however, one plans to make frames only once in a great while, it will be found most economical to go to a regular lumber company dealing in builder's Moldings. These are available in a considerable range of profiles and sizes and are used for the "trim" in house building. With an inexpensive strip of wood of various thicknesses and widths attached to the back to form a rabbet, suitable Moldings can easily be made for picture frames.

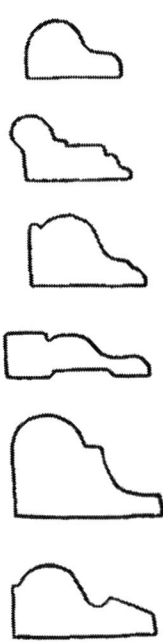

The strip attached to the back to form the rabbet should be at least ¼" thick and of the correct width to make the rabbet about ⅜" deep. It should be attached properly by glue and clamps only, but if it is necessary to nail it, be sure to avoid cutting into the nails and dulling the saw when the molding is cut into the right lengths.

Some builder's Moldings are sufficiently thick so that the lumber yard can cut a rabbet directly into the stock.

These Moldings can naturally be decorated and finished like any other molding although it will be found that the wood *is* distinctly uneven in quality and consequently harder to work. There will also be slightly more waste through the discard of defective pieces. But for your first efforts it will provide an economical method of experimentation.

READY-MADE RAW WOOD PICTURE FRAMES

If sufficient elementary wood-working tools are not owned and investment in them is not desired until it is seen what can be done with finishing, it is wisest to buy frames ready-made to size in raw wood. Any picture framer will make them up, but if standard sizes can be used many art stores carry them in stock at lower prices. This is a recent development and an expanding industry. Only a few rasps or carving tools, brushes, tin cans and jars are all the equipment needed for finishing.

At any rate, it is advised that one compare prices and select the method or source for frames which best fills one's needs and which is most economical.

Complete directions on how to construct frames by various methods, and full descriptions of basic finishes are presented in the following sections.

CHAPTER FOUR

MITER *CUTTING*

To TEACH THE USE of Woodworking tools or any mechanical process without an actual demonstration involves many words. While the following has been made as concise as possible, repetition of rules may be found. Wherever it does occur it is because certain simple practices to produce good work are overlooked only too often.

The arrangement of the working quarters for miter cutting and joining is important. There should be a strong bench attached to the floor if possible, shelves for finishing materials and a convenient rack for tools. An efficient arrangement will surely reduce errors in measuring and cutting besides making for better workmanship generally. Once everything *is* in its place, proceed in an orderly fashion to do the work and replace all tools and equipment when finished.

If several frames are being made at once, complete each step for all the frames before proceeding to the next operation. Measure and mark all the molding strips, cut them into sections, cut the miters, size the joints with glue, etc. Naturally, if frames are being made regularly or a great many are to be made at one time, it will be more efficient to divide the work into groups. Measure, cut and miter all of one size or type first and then another.

When cutting miters preparatory to joining, the

beginner is bound to make errors and to experience a certain amount of waste. Much expensive molding can be saved if experiments are conducted with pieces of scrap wood. The first attempts in frame-making should consist of cutting perfect miters, making strong, tight joints and then cutting wood to predetermined lengths. The small amount of effort and time spent in practicing will be quickly repaid.

Care and good craftsmanship in frame-making have no substitutes. The experience gained in woodworking by solving framing problems in a functional way and actually making frames will gradually develop the faculty of choosing the correct profile of molding for each picture.

Before starting to cut the miters, it will be necessary to have a gauge of some sort attached to the miter box, provided the combination tool (which comes with a gauge) has not been purchased. No amount of careful marking will take the place of a measuring gauge and stop-block for cutting Moldings accurately to specified, equal lengths.

A yardstick, a small C-clamp and a block of wood,

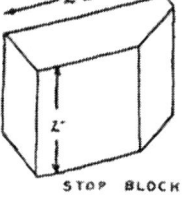

STOP BLOCK

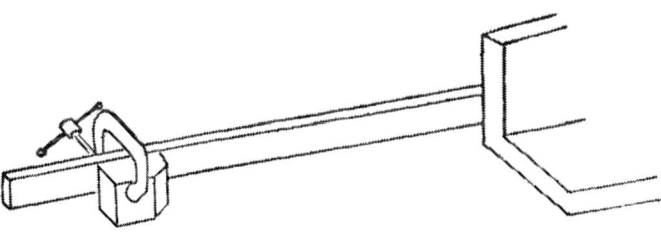

STOP BLOCK

35

one end of which is mitered are all that is necessary to construct a primitive gauge that can be attached or removed quickly from the miter box. Suitable extensions can be attached easily to accommodate larger frames.

The yardstick itself will have to be mitered at one end and then attached to the back of the miter box while the saw is in position for cutting. The simple stop-block should be thick enough to take up the difference between the fence and the yardstick. Only enough of the block needs to be mitered to make for accurate measuring. When clamping it at a particular point, be sure that it is vertical. Once a cut has been made with it in position for one side of a frame, do not shift it until the other piece has been cut.

Before using the miter box and gauge for the first time with regular molding, try making practice cuts with scrap wood but remember that the depth of the rabbet will have to be taken into account. The attachment described is a rather crude affair and is shown

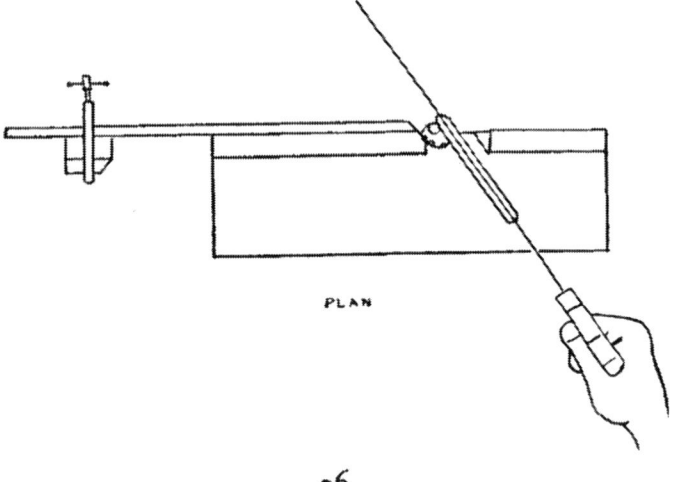

PLAN

36

merely to illustrate the necessity for such a device. More efficient gauges will undoubtedly suggest themselves and should be worked out until they are as accurate as possible with the particular miter box being used.

The selection of molding is the first preparation **for** cutting the four sides of the frame. Always discard badly warped sections or those with other faults. The discarded pieces should be saved, however, for experi-

mentation with decoration or for samples. It is a good plan, also, to cut the longest sides of the frame from the straightest and best parts of a length of molding. By measuring carefully and spacing the pieces properly, waste can be reduced to a minimum. It will be found occasionally that after four sides have been marked from a piece of molding, the remaining section is just too short to be of any real use. To avoid this waste, particularly with the wider Moldings, it is more economical to cut three of the sides from one length of molding and the fourth from another.

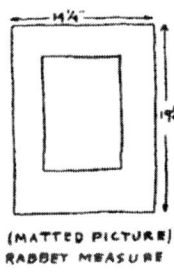

(MATTED PICTURE)
RABBET MEASURE

At this point it is necessary to decide which of the two methods of measuring a picture for a frame is to be used. Matted pictures, prints or drawings or stretched canvases are more economically measured by taking the RABBET measure. This is the length that the back of the rabbet will be after the miters are cut, allowing, of course, extra for insertion of the picture. On the other hand, assuming that a picture painted

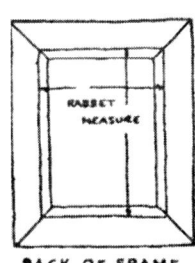

BACK OF FRAME

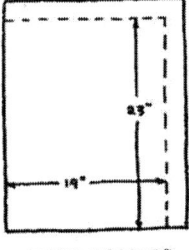

SIGHT MEASURE

on a panel measuring 20" x 24" is to be framed but that only an area measuring 19" x 23" be shown, it would call for SIGHT measure. This would be the measurement along the *inside* edge of the frame.

Whichever method is used the molding will be marked in the same manner because the beginner should not at this time attempt to take into consideration the depth of the rabbet. A little waste when first cutting miters is preferable to spoilage of a frame through inaccurate marking.

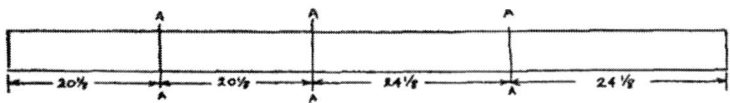

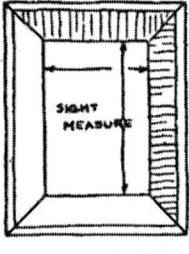

FRONT OF FRAME

The first operation before actually cutting the miters is to mark the molding for cutting the four pieces straight across. (AA in drawing) This will make the work easier to handle. It is at this point that beginners are apt to make their first serious error because the *width* of the molding is not taken into consideration. Whether sight or rabbet measure is used, *always* add *twice* the width of the molding to the actual size of the picture *plus* enough to allow for insertion. This rule cannot be emphasized too strongly, so check and re-check before cutting.

Lay the length of molding face up on the bench with the rabbet side facing away. Assuming that the molding is 2" wide over-all and that a frame for a picture 16" x 20" is to be made. First add about ⅛" to the measurements to allow for insertion of the picture. Then add twice the width of the molding

38

(4") to each measurement. The lengths that the molding is to be cut into are now 20⅛ x 24⅛". After the molding has been marked and checked, it is sawn across from the top to bottom. Any splitting will therefore occur on the rabbet side and will be discarded with the waste from the miter cut.

Allow more or less extra for insertion or "play" for each particular job. For instance, space for insertion will necessarily be limited according to the depth of the rabbet. Again, on frames for stretched canvases or wooden panels, the extra length and width may be as much as ¼" to allow for contraction and expansion.

Another important rule to remember when cutting miters is that the molding must be held firmly so that it does not shift in the miter box. In addition, it must be placed absolutely flat against the base of the miter box, otherwise the miter will be cut at an angle to the molding and will not join. The sketch shows exaggerated cuts.

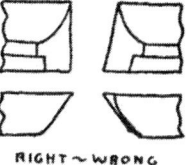

RIGHT ~ WRONG

Place the piece to be mitered in the box, face up, and with the rabbet side toward the front. The saw guide should be swung to the *hit.* Hold or clamp the molding firmly, insert the saw and bringing it down slowly start the cut. Proceed to cut one end off all four pieces in this fashion.

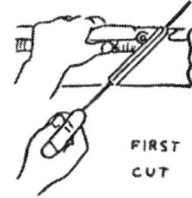

FIRST CUT

Next swing the saw guide to the *light* and attach the gauge. Set the stop-block at the proper point for cutting the *longest* sides first. Make the cuts as before but reverse the molding so that the rabbet is toward the back. Check the two lengths by placing them back to back. Unless they are exactly the same length, it is useless to overlook the fact and proceed

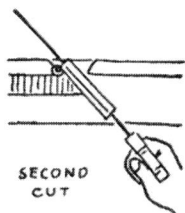

SECOND CUT

39

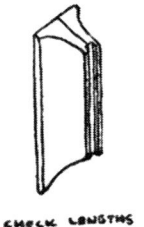

CHECK LENGTHS

to join them later. The frame will not only be wider on one side than another, but it will be impossible to make tightly fitting, accurately joined corners. The gauge should now be set for the two shorter lengths and the miters cut on them, checking the lengths as before.

Cutting for rabbet measure will make the "sight" of the frame smaller and cutting for sight measure will make the back of the rabbet longer.

A method for securing true miters, before the introduction of accurate miter boxes and mass-production tools for picture frames, was by the use of "shooting" boards. Miters were first cut quite roughly and later planed down to the exact length by using the boards. It was a good method in the hands of a skilled woodworker, but its use is not really necessary today provided cuts are made accurately with the miter box. The beginner, using a shooting-board, is apt to plane too much off first one end and then the other trying to make them equal. Something like sawing off first one leg of a tipping table and then another until there is nothing left. When a need for one is felt, a homemade affair will work just as well as an expensive, ready-made shooting-board equipped with a plane.

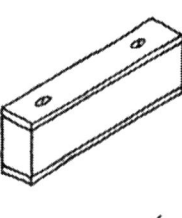

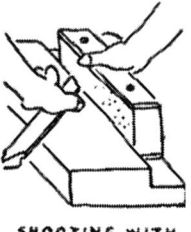

SHOOTING WITH
THE BLOCK

A shooting-board employing sandpaper instead of a plane will be found to give very smooth surfaces for excellent gluing work and will not remove enough of the wood so that the length is appreciably affected.

All that is required *is* one piece of wood 1" x 8" x 20" and another 1" x 6" x 20" fastened on top with one edge flush. On top of the assembly are fastened two small pieces, 1" x 1", as shown. They must be attached

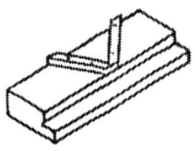

at exactly 45^0 to the top piece, otherwise the sanding block will cut the miter at a wrong angle thus preventing proper joining. Screw all parts together for durability.

The sanding block must be square and smooth. A piece of fir or pine 2" x 3" and 8" long will be suitable. It is necessary to make a clamping arrangement to hold the sandpaper smooth so that it will not have to be wrapped entirely around the block. Clamps to hold the paper can be easily made by cutting two pieces of wood ½" thick, 1¾" wide and 8" long. Place the paper around the block and fasten the two pieces to the top and bottom with ¾" countersunk screws.

Shooting-boards do not usually prove to be necessary except for certain woods or if the saw makes a very rough cut.

CHAPTER FIVE

JOINING THE FRAME

THREE THINGS DISTINGUISH the well-made frame from the careless job. First, the sides are cut exactly the same length so that after the frame is joined, each corner will make a true square. Second, the miters must be cut at a perfect angle of 45^0 and be absolutely vertical or 90^0 to the length and thirdly, there must be perfect joining; the miters must meet with no projecting edges. With constant attention to these three requirements the beginner will find it easier to produce good frames.

At the same time that Moldings are being cut and joined, sample corners should be made from waste pieces. It will be apparent that these corners will be extremely useful for testing various styles of Moldings and finishes with pictures before deciding on frames. Very often only a slight variation in decoration or finish will make a particular molding suitable for a number of totally different pictures. Narrow Moldings made up into sample corners will be found useful as inserts for wider Moldings to make the latter more interesting and important or to test contrasts in finishes.

Nailing is usually the operation which gives the beginner the most trouble. The secret lies in drilling the hole in the first piece large enough for a sliding fit and in not making the hole too deep in the adjoining length. Long nails are apt to bend when driving, so extra care should be used with them. Never strike too heavy a blow with the hammer because it may loosen the glued joint and drive it out of square. The beginner who has not practiced woodworking will find some difficulty at first as is to be expected. This is more the result of lack of care and accuracy than an inability to handle tools.

Remember that the work will be facilitated and made more accurate if the miter box, miter vise and similar tools can be attached permanently to the work bench. If the bench is needed for other purposes, however, they should be firmly clamped when in use.

After the molding has been cut and the lengths checked, the frame is ready to be joined. All mitered corners are given a very thin coat of glue which is allowed to sink into the wood and become quite dry. Take one short length and one long one (being careful not to join the two short or the two long sides together) and give one piece a second and substantial coat of glue, being careful not to spread the glue too near the top of the molding. Now bring the corners together and either clamp them along the edges of the bench or place them in a miter vise or cramping tool. See that the corner meets perfectly and test for square ness with the try-square.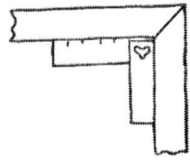

The correct size nails should then be selected by holding them across the corner to see whether they are long enough. Decide at what points they should be driven in by spacing them so that one is driven close to the rabbet, one near the top outside edge and

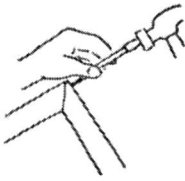

another, from the opposite side, near the bottom outside or between the first two. Place the proper size drill in the hand drill and bore holes just deep enough to penetrate one side. Practice will soon enable one to gauge just how deep the holes should be. Insert the nails in position and drive them almost home from *both* sides. Then, using the nail set, sink the heads of the nails just below the surface. The depth to which they should be sunk depends on the thickness of the frame, but even on very heavy moldings, ⅛" is deep enough. With a damp cloth, wipe off any excess glue which may have been squeezed out. It is difficult to remove after it has dried.

A common error made by beginners when joining is to bore the hole so that when nails are driven in from opposite sides, they strike each other. Try to place the nails to give the maximum holding power and always at an angle; the first and longest nail as close to the inside of the rabbet as possible. It is usually necessary to use two or more different sizes of nails for each molding.

After the two sides of the frame are joined, repeat with the other two pieces. The next operation requires careful handling since the joints which have been made must hold by themselves while the last two are completed. With the exception of small frames or rather heavy molding it is necessary in most cases to support the joined corners until the frame is completed. Different thicknesses of wood or tapered blocks made especially for the purpose should be used so that there is no danger of sagging or of joining the frame while it is out of true. These precautions

44

are not necessary if the frame is resting on a perfectly flat surface while it is being joined. After the supporting pieces have raised the frame to the proper height, sight across it, first from one corner and then another to make sure one side is not higher than another. Proceed to finish the joining carefully, wiping off any excess glue as before. Lay the frame on a flat surface and allow the glue to set for a few hours before doing any more work on it. If several frames are being made at once, it will be found that the first frame completed will be ready for more work by the time they have all been joined.

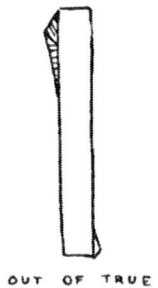

OUT OF TRUE

In spite of care being exercised to avoid joining the frame while all sides are not level, it may occasionally not lie flat. This may be caused by an imperceptible twist or warp in the molding itself. Should it occur, lay the frame face down before the glue has set and drive in wooden wedges to spread the back of two of the joints until the frame lies flat and does not rock. After the glue has dried, cut off the excess wedges and smooth down.

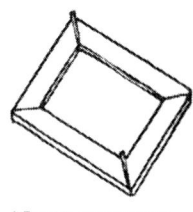

DRIVES WEDGES IN
BACK OF 2 CORNERS

The method described is a standard, simple way of joining frames. There are many others involving the use of spline joints, dowels, etc., which deserve consideration, although their use is largely unnecessary except in the case of very wide, flat Moldings or exceptionally heavy frames for mirrors.

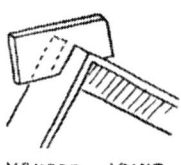

SAW CUT

The first and easiest *is* the veneer joint. The frame is first cramped together with glue using one or another of the cramping tools described and allowed to set, preferably from four to six hours. One or more saw cuts are then made across each of the corners and

VENEER JOINT

45

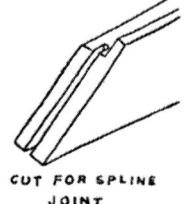

CUT FOR SPLINE
JOINT

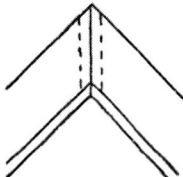

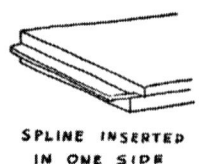

SPLINE INSERTED
IN ONE SIDE

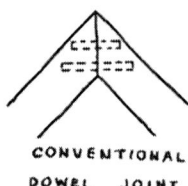

CONVENTIONAL
DOWEL JOINT

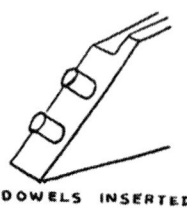

DOWELS INSERTED
IN ONE SIDE

thin strips of veneer as thick as the kerf of the saw with the grain running at right angles to that of the frame are inserted after being given a coat of glue. After drying, the projecting edges are carefully cut off and the corners smoothed with sandpaper. Holes can then be bored and nails or screws inserted for added strength.

The spine joint requires the use of a power bench saw or a sawing jig to insure accuracy of the saw cut. The cut to receive the strip of wood called a spine is made in each corner before the frame is joined. The spines must be made the exact thickness of the saw kerf and must have the grain running at right angles to the wood of the molding.

After the miter has been glued, the spine is also coated heavily and inserted in one side. The corners are then brought together and joined with nails as described previously. The edges which project are smoothed off after drying.

Dowel joints for frames are not too difficult to accomplish if the dowel is permitted to run directly through at least one side of the frame and smoothed off later. However, common practice is to drill two or more holes in one piece to a certain depth, insert dowel points to locate the holes on the other piece and then drill them at the same angle. Needless to say, this method requires some cabinet-making skill, and it seems doubtful whether enough additional strength is gained to warrant the work involved. As an alternative, it suggested that the holes for the dowels be bored in either of two ways; through one side or through both. A dowel of the correct size is then given a liberal coat of glue and driven home.

46

After the glue has set, cut off the dowel ends and smooth flush with the molding. The dowels will be invisible after painting or gilding the frame. Nails or screws are usually not necessary.

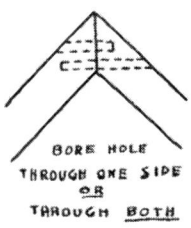

Still another method is to join the frame in the regular way and then to cut a groove across the back. A strip of wood, well glued, is then inserted and nailed down. It is obvious that this type of joint will not add much additional reinforcement because the strip has only three bearing surfaces.

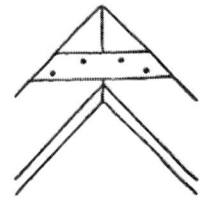

At times, on very wide frames, it is the practice to attach a triangular piece of wood across the back of each corner after the frame has been assembled, ¼ plywood is the best wood for the purpose and after it has been attached, the edges are planed down to a sharp angle.

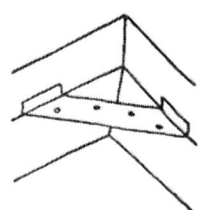

Unless the reinforcement of the mitered corner joint occurs near the front or top of the frame (where the real stress takes place) little is to be gained by the additional work involved.

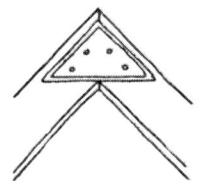

Because wood can never be worked to the precision of metal, it will be discovered that no matter how high the quality of molding purchased nor the amount of care used in cutting the miters, there will be slight variations when the parts are joined. Either the inside, the outside or some other part will not be absolutely flush, that is, the two pieces will never meet perfectly at every spot. Some of this tendency can be overcome by allowing the irregularity to occur at the back of the frame by raising or lowering one piece in the vise until the joint appears as perfect as possible from the front. After the frame has been joined, examine each corner carefully and carve or sandpaper the differences away until the joint is smooth. After sanding the whole frame, fill all dents, flaws, cracks and nail-holes with "crack-filler". The use of this material is recommended instead of the various "plastic" wood compounds because it is easier to work; it is also cheaper because only enough need be mixed for each project and it is better because it will not shrink when dry. For natural wood finishes or on pre-finished molding, the crack-filler can be colored with casein colors to the desired shade.

In spite of using the very best of well-seasoned molding and the utmost care in making joints, after varying lengths of time tiny cracks will appear at the miters through the finish of the frame. Sometimes the cracks will not appear for many years, but steam-heated apartments usually hasten the process. This is not due to any fault in the making or finishing of the frame but occurs because all wood keeps oxidizing or drying out and shrinking. In time, even the filling of the nail holes will be forced loose. If any antique frame *is* examined, it will be seen that the filling of the nail or screw holes protrudes above the level of the wood.

Occasionally one has a frame on hand which is too large for a particular picture but otherwise suitable. While it is usually more satisfactory to refinish all frames which have been cut down, sometimes for the sake of saving time, the frame can be so cut that it can be reassembled without spoiling all four corners. Let us assume that we have a frame measuring 24" x 30" to be cut down to 20" x 22".

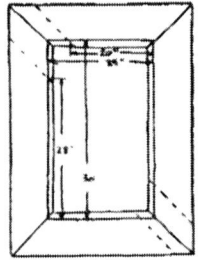

First measure along the inside of the rabbet of the 30" side and mark it at 22". Using a 45^0 angle, draw a miter to the outside edge of the frame and mark it where the angle intersects. Repeat the process on the 24" side, marking it at 20". Clamp the frame in the *vise* at a point where the saw will cut at the mark and sever the frame after making an adjustment on the gauge for the opposite side. Be sure supports are under the forms at all times so that the side not held in the *vise* will be prevented from falling down suddenly and thus break the corner that is to be saved. Lift the frame out carefully, holding the cut part together and repeat with the shorter side. Next replace the part still retaining the waste pieces, check the gauge, and cut off the part to be discarded. Only two corners need to be put together, the joints smoothed and touched up to match the finish. This method will be found particularly useful when cutting down second-hand frames, especially those with heavy ornamentation.

If all the corners show signs of being loose, it is advisable gently to separate the entire frame, even if nails must be cut through. Cut all the miters fresh (avoiding nails) and reassemble. Keep the scrap pieces as samples if the finish is to be duplicated exactly, but consider the frame as raw. Clean it by washing and sand it down to give it tooth. It is not necessary to remove the old finish completely provided it is not waxed or greasy.

Ornaments or other decorations are sometimes spoiled when cutting down frames. Some of these can be glued back into place or small parts simulated with

49

crack-filler. In case a large piece on an elaborate frame needs to be replaced however, it is better to take a casting of a duplicate section in plaster of paris and fit it in. The procedure described in the section on repairing has been found practical.

IN THE SOUTH *by*
THOMAS H. BENTON

This frame shows the use of a plain linen insert. Its employment keeps the rather strong decoration from being too distracting. The frame itself is a good illustration of how abstract decoration, rather than tiresome naturalistic forms, aids in the presentation of a picture.

SAINT PAUL
LIPPO MEMMI

Early 14th Century Italian

An excellent example of the period. The frame is not only part of the picture but carries out the spirit of the composition as well. Experimentation in framing contemporary pictures along this idea might be in order.

PORTRAIT OF A MAN
DIRK BOUTS

Early 15th Century Flemish

This can hardly be called a frame for a picture. It is rather a piece of sculptured architecture with a window in it. Strangely enough, finished as it is in gold and placed in its proper setting, it is probably perfect.

NEEDLEPOINT PORTRAIT
ARTIST UNKNOWN
17th Century

The texture of the decoration on this frame is exceptionally well suited to the picture. The general effect would be better, however, if the frame had a mat finish. So many highlights are disturbing and unnecessary.

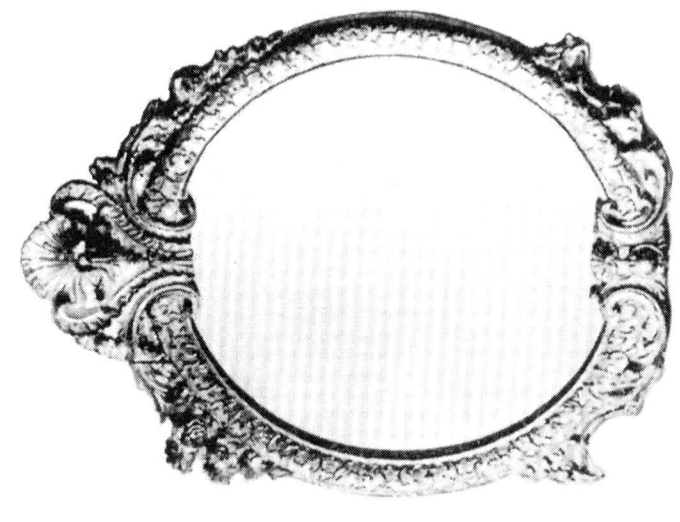

LOUIS XVI   REGENCY STYLE

Early 18th Century French

This oval frame is only one of the endless variations of the same idea characteristic of this period. They all followed the same style of having a top-heavy central ornament and too much decoration. There was no attempt to integrate frames with pictures.

HOLY FAMILY *by* ANDREA MANTEGNA

Early 16th Century Italian

A rather elaborate version of the "Doorway" type of frame. The ornamentation derived from naturalistic sources, seems bad. It may be that this frame was a later attempt to imitate the earlier, simpler examples.

PORTRAIT OF A MAN by REMBRANDT

Frames of this "Barbizon" type naturally lend importance to a picture. It is a current practice among picture dealers to put contemporary paintings in such frames for just this purpose. The practice seems wrong because the frame is so overpowering that it interferes with seeing the picture.

MRS. JOHN BIDDLE by THOMAS SULLY

The corner decorations of this frame are well executed. They are not as overly elaborate as their European counterparts. Note the modification of the egg and dart motif on the inner edge. The whole frame is uninspired but has taste and good simplicity, considering the period.

1   2

WOMAN IN WHITE   by *PICASSO*

1. This is one solution for the problem of framing reproductions inexpensively. The raw wood frame was very simply finished by giving it a wash of white casein paint, sanding and waxing. It is interesting, when comparing these photographs, to note how very much the style of a frame can help to create an illusion of different picture sizes.

2. Before remodeling, this was a very heavy, ornamented gilt frame. The ornaments on the top edge, which made the frame very deep, were knocked off. The simple decorations were then cut with a round file. It was given the finish described as "Antique Finish No. 1." Compare the photograph with the others also designed by the author for the same picture.

3

4

3. Unfortunately, one view of this frame cannot give the three-dimensional quality it possesses. It projects the picture from the wall and can be adapted, with modifications of width and depth, to many pictures. The author believes that there is a need for more experimentation in frame design along this line. Frames will then eventually be created which will not only harmonize with the picture but with the architecture of the room in which it is to hang.

4. A fairly wide and deep angle frame illustrating simple texturing on the inside edge. It is a good illustration of how a frame will make a picture appear larger. It was designed by the author as a more or less standard profile, the finish harmonizing with each picture.

REDHEAD WITH POODLE   by MARCEL VERTES

The shallow, abstract carving on this frame combined with the rubbed effect is an interesting method of finishing a frame. The photograph makes it appear quite heavy and overpowering, but properly finished, it is very harmonious.

VIADUCT   *by FEININGER*

This modern frame is finished in silver leaf. It is excellent in design and proportion and enhances the picture beautifully. The highlights and reflections repeat the planes of the picture with perfect results. Such good framing is rare.

VALLEY   *by FREDERIC TAUBES*

An excellent example of straight combing texture on a wide and deep scoop molding. The decoration on the edge is good but perhaps would be better if it were less "busy." However, the color of the finish and the linen insert pulls the whole together.

HULL ASSEMBLY – PBY
by JOHN McCRADY

Note how the beading has been decorated on this frame with a few simple cuts. The straight combing texture is satisfying and the wide, coarse-textured, extra-thick mat very useful for certain pictures. In this case, however, a narrower mat would have strengthened the picture.

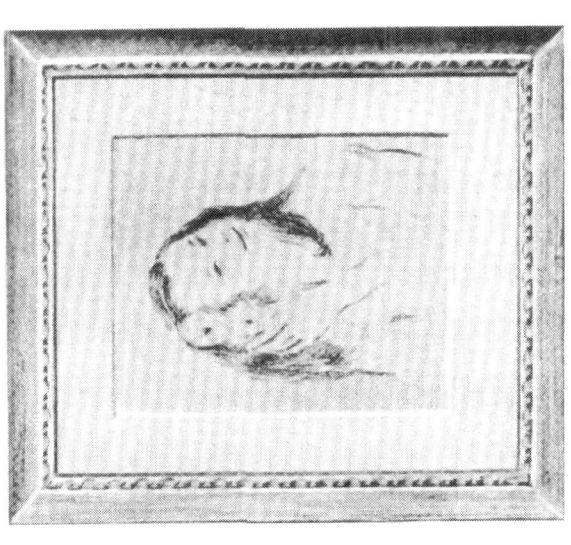

GIRL WITH CAMELIAS
by MARCEL VERTES

The restrained use of decoration on this frame is very pleasing. There is just enough of it to relieve the severity of the shallow scoop-moulding used. It seems almost a rule that the simpler the treatment, provided the finish is harmonious, the better.

TREE   *by JOHN STEUART CURRY*

This frame has many admirable qualities but it might have been even more successful if the combing texture had been next to the carved beading and the outside left plain. The edge next to the linen insert might have been left undecorated. The effect then would have been more unified. The practice of alternating plain and decorated parts of a frame was a bad fault of the Victorian era.

CIRCUS CHILD WITH HORSE
by MARCEL VERTES

The very thick mat which is well-proportioned to the picture and the running decoration make this a good example of a conventional, contemporary solution to a framing problem. Note the treatment of the corners and how much more successful individualized decoration of this sort is compared to ready-made mouldings.

HEAD   by UMBERTO ROMANO

Deep in tonal value, but with a light wash, this frame complements the picture perfectly. The light-colored insert also helps considerably. The picture would have appeared larger, however, if the width of the fillet had been made smaller.

UNDER THE HILL BUCK   by *JOHN McCRADY*

The use of a beveled insert painted a very light color is well illustrated in this example. The plain scoop molding has been given a coarse surface and the edge decorated with a conventionalized egg-and-dart motif. A useful treatment for small pictures.

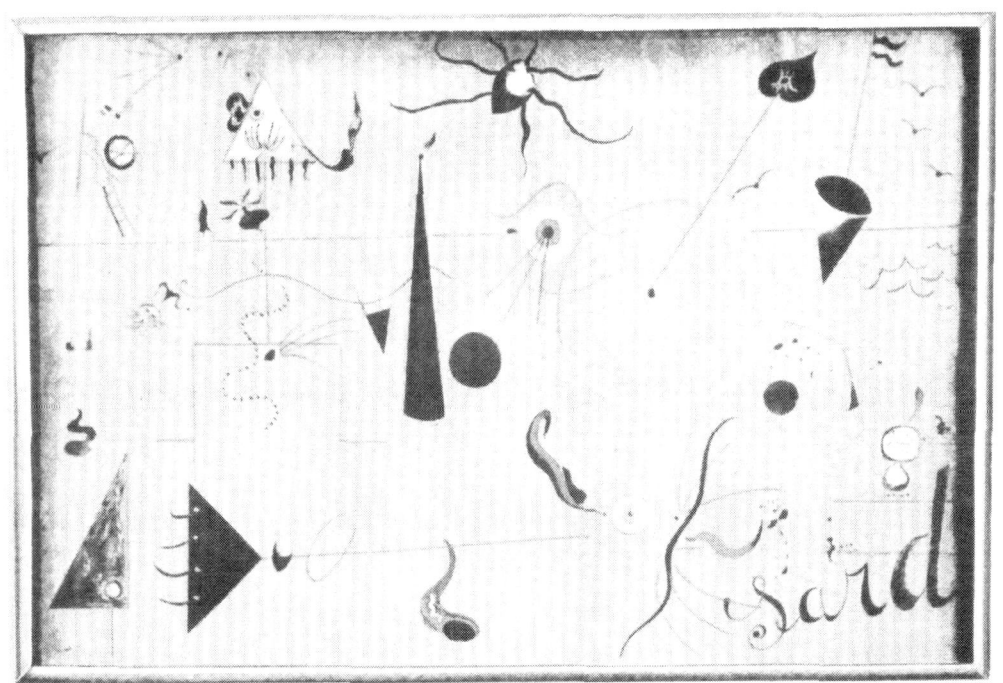

CATALAN LANDSCAPE   *by MIRO*

The frame does not "bind" the picture but does form a good boundary for its areas. It is an example of simple, contemporary framing that should be more prevalent. The frame is not deep and is only rounded on its outside edge.

GIRL WITH PARROT by MARCEL VERTES

The decoration, equalized from the centers of the sides, gives this frame a handsome, crisp appearance. It is, in reality, three frames in one and a very fine treatment for this particular picture. The light color gives it a pleasing quality and while the frame is wide and relatively heavy, it does not dominate the picture.

CHAPTER SIX

INSERTS *(Or Linings)*

INSERTS ARE FRAMES within frames. They are used either to make the molding appear heavier and wider, to form a decorative border next to the picture or to reduce the size of larger frames to fit smaller pictures. With ingenuity, an insert can be fitted to a frame which, because of its size and shape, seemed impossible for use with a particular picture. Several methods of making, covering and finishing inserts are described in the following.

The most common insert in use is a plain, flat, rounded or beveled molding of any width from ¼ up. Inserts over 2" wide, however, give the effect of a mat but if they have their own rabbet are technically inserts no matter what the width. The plain insert can be gilded, bronzed, painted or decorated to harmonize or contrast with the frame. When covered with natural linen or monkscloth, it will be found very useful because of the neutral tone of these fabrics. Other textiles may also be used with exceptionally fine effects for certain pictures.

Inserts, carved or decorated with a continuous motif of a simple pattern, can also be used to form a decorative border inside the frame. It is obvious that because it will be next to the picture, the decoration should be unobtrusive and should merely complement the frame.

51

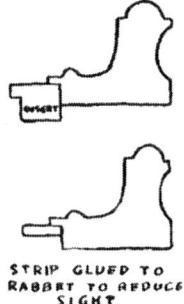

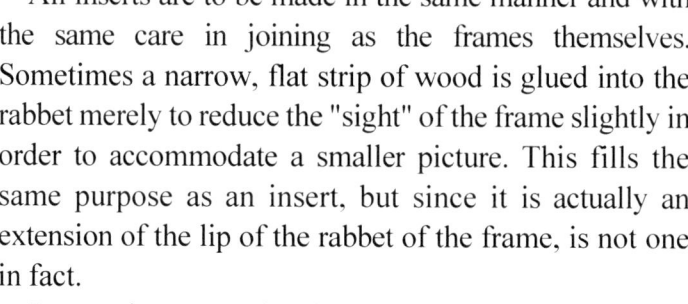

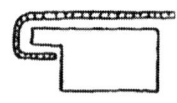

STRIP GLUED TO
RABBET TO REDUCE
SIGHT

All inserts are to be made in the same manner and with the same care in joining as the frames themselves. Sometimes a narrow, flat strip of wood is glued into the rabbet merely to reduce the "sight" of the frame slightly in order to accommodate a smaller picture. This fills the same purpose as an insert, but since it is actually an extension of the lip of the rabbet of the frame, is not one in fact.

Inserts do not need to be made of the finest molding stock if they are to be covered with a fabric. They do not even need to be smoothed with sandpaper. There are two popular methods of covering inserts with cloth. The first, and the easiest with which to produce clean joints, is to cover each piece of the molding separately and then to do the joining. The other is to make the insert as a complete frame, covering it later and mitering the corners carefully. In the case of heavy cloth or pile fabrics, the latter method is preferable.

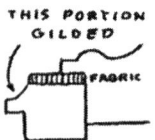

THIS PORTION
GILDED

FABRIC

Inserts are frequently attractive when they are not completely covered with cloth, but combined with a painted stripe of color or gilt. For instance, the inside edge and part of the top of the insert could so be finished. Velvet *is* available in ribbon form with finished edges and in varying width and colors. It *is* easily applied ⅛" or more from the edge and will present a neatly finished appearance. The darker colors combined with a gold line give a particularly rich effect.

It is advisable to experiment with textiles of different colors and weaves to see what type may be most suited to the picture before attempting to cover the insert. Be sure to save scraps of textiles which may have been used for covering inserts. They will be useful as samples for future work.

Neatness and precision must be especially observed when adhering cloth to inserts. Do not use too much glue and never press the cloth down too hard or the glue will be forced through it. It is almost impossible to remove cabinet glue which has touched the face of the fabric without leaving a stain or spoiling the work completely. Velvet or plush in particular are fragile and must be handled carefully in order not to crush the material too much. The pile will naturally be forced down somewhat when gluing, but a clothes brush will bring it up properly.

To cover an insert using the first method mentioned, first cut the fabric into strips long enough and wide enough to cover the four pieces as shown. Take one of the pieces of molding to be used for the insert (which has been cut to the proper length less two thicknesses of the material to be used) and lay it face down. Incidentally, when using a heavy fabric such as monkscloth, l/g" will have to be allowed. Spread hot cabinet glue on the *bottom of the lip* of the rabbet. Attach one of the strips of the fabric to the glued surface, pressing it down with a piece of wood or metal always keeping the fabric straight. It will be discovered quickly exactly what shape and kind of implement is needed for the work. Attach one edge of each of the pieces of cloth to the other three sides and lay them aside to dry. Now lay the first piece on its back with the rabbet facing away. Coat the top of the molding with hot glue and, pulling it gently

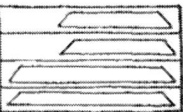

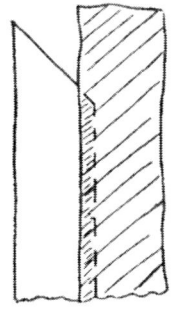

INSERT FACE DOWN
FABRIC FACE UP

53

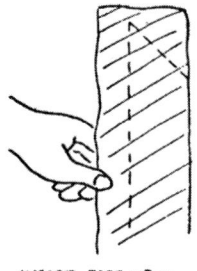

INSERT FACE UP —
PULL FABRIC OVER

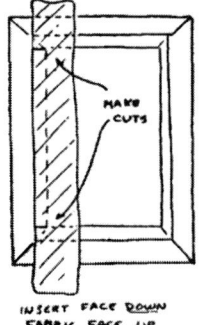

MAKE
CUTS

INSERT FACE DOWN
FABRIC FACE UP

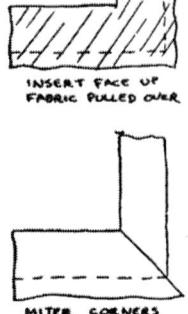

INSERT FACE UP
FABRIC PULLED OVER

MITER CORNERS

back, press the fabric down so that it will be flat and free from wrinkles. Next coat the mitered corners, and after making the proper cuts in the material, glue down the ends snugly. After each piece has been covered in this way, the excess material is trimmed off when the glue is dry and the four pieces are joined like a frame. Extreme care must be used so that glue will not be forced up on top of the fabric at the joints. Apply the glue at least ¼" below the top edge on each miter. While the mitered joints are very obvious on this type of insert, the neatness and speed makes them quite satisfactory.

A more attractive way of covering inserts but one which requires more skill, is to assemble the insert completely and then cover it. As before, first cut the four strips of fabric with plenty to spare. Lay the insert face down and proceed to cover two *opposite* sides as described above, making cuts in the cloth so that it will not wrinkle when folding it over. Be careful when applying the glue to the top not to extend it beyond the mitered corner of the insert. Now take a small ruler and make the miter cut to follow exactly that of the frame. Turn the insert on its face again and repeat the operation for the other two sides. The final operation, and the one requiring the greatest care, is the cutting of the overlapping material so that perfect corners are assured. After pressing the last two sides down, try to find the ridge of the material beneath and make the miter cut with a razor blade directly over the first two. This method of covering inserts is the most satisfactory for heavy material.

Still a third way of covering is to take a piece of

54

material ½" to 1" larger than the joined insert, lay it down and place the insert face down on it. Cut out the center after marking it carefully so that enough is left to glue to the rabbet, and attach the inside edges first. Turn the insert over and proceed to glue down the top. While this type of covering is exceptionally handsome, there is a considerable amount of waste. It is useful for small pictures but because of the care which is needed to achieve a neat finish, it should not be attempted by the beginner until he has gained some experience.

INSERT FACE DOWN

Inserts can also be sprayed with flocking which is a powdered textile material to give the effect of cloth or they can be textured or carved to match the frame. Inserts invariably add to the finished appearance and interest of most frames. They also, where needed, help separate the picture from the frame.

CUT ON HEAVY LINES

Let us assume that one has an excellent frame which has a sight measure of 24½" by 29". Further, that one has a canvas measuring 24" by 30". To the amateur, it may seem a hopeless task because if the picture is cut down in length, it will still be too narrow. If the frame is cut down in width, it will still be too short. The solution to such a problem is to employ an insert. First cut the rabbet of the frame to accommodate the length of the canvas. In this case, ½" or more will have to be routed out with chisel and rabbet plane to make the rabbet dimension of the frame 30" long and 24½" wide plus room for insertion of the canvas. Next take the measurement to determine the narrowest possible strip necessary to hold the picture along the 30" sides. The illustration shows the re-

GLUE ALL INSIDE EDGES FIRST

CHISEL OUT SHADED AREA

55

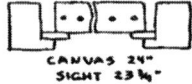

CANVAS 24"
SIGHT 23¾"

quired width. Make four strips of wood, ⅛" or 3/16"thick, long enough to cover all four sides. Cut the miters carefully and nail and glue the strips into place so that an equal amount of each shows from the front. After the glue is dry, finish to match or contrast with the frame. It is true that a small part of each end of the picture is cut from sight by using this device, but much time and labor is saved.

Remember that the frame which is designed to have an insert must take its rabbet measurement from the outside edge of the insert. To avoid mistakes, it is suggested that the insert be made first and then the frame cut to the proper size.

Other materials such as sheet cork, metal, etc., will occur to one for use in covering inserts. Inserts will be found to be of the utmost value to the framer because they frequently make the all-important transition from picture to frame easy and harmonious. Their use should always be considered before a final decision is reached on the frame for any picture.

CHAPTER SEVEN

FINISHES

AT FIRST GLANCE, this section may appear considerably extended in relation to the rest of die book. It is detailed because it is the finish which will ultimately make or break the frame. No matter how well constructed, designed or decorated a frame may be, an inharmonious finish will ruin the final effect.

The sound rules of good wood finishing also apply to picture frames but unlike furniture or floors, the finishes need not be as durable. For example, a simple shellac or lacquer finish, waxed, is just as satisfactory for a natural wood frame as a carefully varnished, rubbed and oiled finish is for furniture. The rules to be observed are, have the frame free from dust, oil or grease before attempting a finish; allow every coat to dry properly before attempting further work and use good materials.

Many new materials for painted finishes are now on the market which replace ones that previously took much time to apply. The most popular for contemporary frame finishing is the new casein water paint. Purchased in a good brand, it will be found extraordinarily easy to use for texturing and as a basic undercoat.

Lacquers come in varying degrees of finish from flat to gloss and of course are unsurpassed for durability and smoothness. Unfortunately, the successful employment of them depends on a spray gun and an air compressor. Literature on the operation of spraying equipment is plentiful and would be superfluous in this volume.

Another new development in the paint field, especially useful for frame finishing, is a flat oil paint designed for application directly over kalsomine or casein finishes. One can do all the basic work on the frame with the fast-drying casein paint and then water-proof it with this type of oil paint.

Shellac, naturally, is a requisite for the frame finisher. Both the white and the orange varieties have their distinct uses and should be kept on hand. However, shellac has the bad property of not drying after it has been kept for long periods of time. Therefore, only small quantities should be purchased at a time or dry shellac should be stored and dissolved in denatured alcohol as needed.

A set of oil colors in tubes or colors ground in oil in cans together with flat white oil paint of good quality will also be necessary.

For texturing, all sorts of implements can be used, but a few steel graining combs with differently spaced teeth, old whiskbrooms and brushes will be found invaluable.

While gilding or bronzing is being used considerably less than in previous years, it is well to be prepared to handle the occasional frame that requires a metallic finish. Satisfactory leaf finishes can be applied without the necessity of elaborate equipment although professional gilding is a skill that requires care and experience. With the substitution of other finishes because of the changed fashion in frames, it should be rarely necessary to use leaf. Directions and materials for gilding will therefore be placed at the end of this section.

The following list of paints, solvents, etc., will be adequate for almost all finishing work. Only purchase them as the need for individual items arises.

> White cast in paste paint
> Casein deep colors: Red, Yellow, Blue, etc.
> White oil paint for use over kalsomine
> Flat white oil paint
> White enamel
> Set of oil colors
> Shellac (white and orange)
> Paste wax
> Flatting oil
> Japan drier
> Water or oil stains for wood
> Bronze powders
> Burnish powders
> Gold Compo XX
> Turpentine, Linseed Oil, Alcohol, Benzine
> Rabbit Skin Glue
> Burnisher

After finishing a frame, the paints used and the order of their application to achieve a certain effect should be written down in a notebook kept for the purpose. Sample corners, which can be made from waste pieces when joining, should be finished and numbered to correspond with the finishes recorded in the notebook. It is extremely difficult to duplicate a finish without a great deal of wasted time and effort unless some record *is* kept. This does not mean that work should be stopped to make a note, but within a reasonable time after a finish has been completed it should be written down, particularly if it involves an individual technique. Some time may pass before a certain effect is needed again, but it *is* all too easy to forget the steps by which it was executed. *Casein* Water Paint:

Because it will be found to be the most useful of paints, both for smooth surfaces and for texturing, casein paint heads the list. It can be applied in a thin wash over stained wood finishes for a pickled effect or in a very heavy consistency for texturing. When a container of white casein paint is purchased, do not attempt to mix the whole can into a creamy, brushing consistency, but take out what is needed for each project, scrape down the insides of the container, level off the paint and keep it covered with a thin layer of water. If it is mixed all at once, it will eventually sink to the bottom as it stands around and will be useless in a short time. The same practice should be followed in caring for the deep colors which are used for tinting. Casein paint can be mixed with a small quantity of spar varnish or glycerin to induce plasticity and to retard drying while it is being textured. If glycerin is added, experiment to find just the amount which barely suits the purpose and do not add any more or the finish will not dry properly.

Casein paint, when properly applied, dries for handling in less than an hour and after about thirty days is reasonably waterproof. However, if a frame painted with casein becomes soiled, it is advisable to clean it with art gum or extra fine sandpaper. It is recommended that protective coatings be applied over casein finishes, and these are described under the individual basic finishes.

After the frame has been made ready any of the finishes described in detail later can be applied successfully and with a minimum amount of effort and time.

As has been stated repeatedly, the aim of good finishing is to produce frames which do not clash with the pictures. Neutral-toned finishes are advocated such as warm or cool grays. It will be discovered that a gray made with raw umber is much more adaptable to pictures generally than one made with either ivory or lamp black. Casein paint usually becomes one of two values lighter when it is dry than when wet. For this reason, it is wise when mixing colors, to allow a swatch of the paint to dry in order to be sure that it is the correct tone. In any case, it is better to err on the side of lighter values than to make the color too dark or intense.

Too strong or dark a gray, except for special purposes, gives an effect of drab muddiness. Try various proportions of white casein to raw umber such as 2 to 1, 3 to 1 or 4 to 1, letting each value dry thoroughly until the most suitable is found.

If it is intended to have the neutral tone lean towards a particular color, it is more satisfactory to use the ready-mixed basic tone as a base and add some color rather than to start with white. The resulting tone will always have a pleasing softness and avoid being too strong. The ready-mixed neutral tone may not only be employed for use as a basic color but thinned out with water in another receptacle, may be used for washes over gilt or stained finishes.

Again, bear in mind that it is a mistake to have too strong a color in any frame; that simple finishes, like simple Moldings, are better for the beginner with which to experiment. The finishes which are described in detail in this section are all designed as basic and should certainly be varied by the individual according to his taste and needs. Texturing:

The idea of putting an interesting surface on a frame through the texture of the paint used in finishing is a relatively modern development. Some old frames are to be found which had wide-mesh cloth like netting glued down to break the flat surface and ornaments applied on top. Today, this effect can be duplicated by using paint textured with combs or brushes. It will be much more durable and is readily refinished if damaged.

Although it is possible to buy a "plastic" oil paint, casein is infinitely preferable even if it does require an additional protective coating. The first quality for texturing which a workable paint should have is body or thickness enough to show the pattern and second, that it should remain wet long enough for experimentation. In order to avoid too thin a body, remove a sufficient quantity of the white casein paste from its container and stirring carefully, add only a small amount of water very slowly until it is of the consistency of very thick cream. A few trials on scrap wood will show whether more water or more paste needs to be added to the mixture.

If it is planned to pattern the frame with a bold texture, careful sanding will not be necessary. It is essential, however, that the frame has an even surface. First give all the frames to be textured a medium heavy coat of casein paint. Let dry and then lay out the articles to be used for texturing such as combs (either professional steel graining combs or broken pieces of ordinary hair combs), an old whiskbroom, pieces of wire brushes, a toothbrush, etc. Each one will give a distinct pattern and the more interesting the texture, the less will be the need for carved decoration. Perhaps it would be well to bear in mind the rule: Reduce the texture according to the amount of decoration and always keep it in relation to the size of the molding.

The scraps of molding left over from cutting or short, useless lengths are ideal for trying out ideas. One can be very original here, but first experiment with some of the textures which have already been proven excellent. While experimenting, if it is discovered that the heavy mixture of paint dries too fast, add a small quantity of glycerine; about 1/2 teaspoon to a pint. Only add enough to the paint so that it retains its moisture long enough to be worked. Also, do not attempt to coat or texture the entire frame at once, but complete each side separately.

For the first try, use a simple, straight combing texture. Coat the piece to be textured and brush it back and forth until a heavy, even coat has been applied. Now take one of the steel combs and holding it at

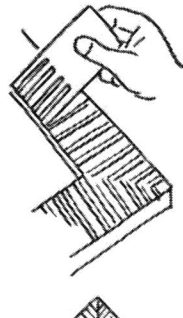

MITER STROKES
AT CORNERS

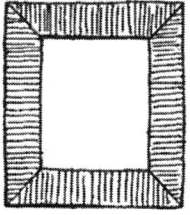

CROSS STROKES

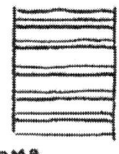

COMB

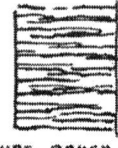

WIRE BRUSH

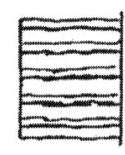

TOOTH BRUSH

an angle, draw it across the molding at right angles to the wood. Place the comb as near as possible to the part just done and repeat along the whole length. This will produce a series of parallel, heavy ridges of different width depending on the size of the comb used. Since the frame must have exactly the same texture all around, some practice will be necessary before one is able to do the mitered corners successfully as shown. Do not expect perfection on the first try. Texturing is relatively easy and it will not be long before professional work is produced. The use of parallel lines of this sort requires a fairly steady stroke and also the ability to sight at right angles across the grain of the wood.

Now, using the same straight, cross stroke, take either the toothbrush or some other stiff, flat brush about 2" wide and repeat the motion. Here, less regularity will be apparent and the lines will flow heavily together in some places and remain distinct in others; the variation adding life to the finish. If the same stroke is done with a small piece of wire brush, still another effect is achieved. The lines will be narrower and sharper and will also bunch up in spots, increasing interest.

The same cross stroke can be tried on a very wide or heavy molding using an old whiskbroom. A new broom can be used, but an old, worn one will give greater variation in the ridges. This texture is heavy and coarse, but is bold and well-suited to wide, simple Moldings.

The next stroke for texturing which has been found useful and successful is the diagonal. With the

64

frame tilted at a comfortable working angle, start at one corner and draw the comb or brush at a 45^0 angle across the molding. It has been found easier on the eye to have the diagonal run from left to right, since that is the natural path of sight. When using the diagonal stroke, always continue around the entire frame so that it has an unbroken effect. Avoid having one side of the frame textured one direction and an adjacent side another. The diagonal stroke is especially good when used on frames with a convex curve because the stroke, combined with the curve, gives a pleasant, rolling effect.

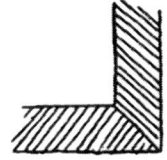

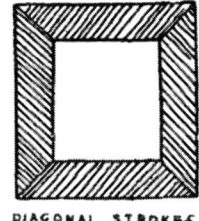

DIAGONAL STROKES

For the last of the straight-line textures, try a stroke running along the length of the molding. On narrow moldings, this will completely eliminate the need for any carved decoration, but one should avoid too heavy or bold a pattern.

Remember that it is by no means necessary to cover the entire frame with texture. It is often extremely effective when either the inside, the outside or only one section of the profile *is* patterned especially if there are sharp edges to separate the parts distinctly.

After practicing all the above exercises and attaining some degree of proficiency, proceed to the texturing strokes involving the use of curved, crossed or combination strokes. Use the steel or hair combs because brushes, unless the strokes are rather widely spaced, tend to obliterate the pattern underneath. Take the narrowest-toothed comb and draw diagonal lines along the length of the molding then cross them at right angles with the widest-toothed comb. It will be seen that while the lines are very prominent in one direction, a definite pattern is created by the pull of the comb last used. This will give something of a snakeskin or textile effect. When using these combinations, make sure that the paint does not dry too fast or it will not show the strokes underneath. Also try brush textures first and wide-toothed combs over them. Endless variations are possible and they will soon express one's individuality in design.

After the straight, cross textures, try some involving a simple curve or S-shape first with straight strokes underneath, crossed by curving, and then reverse the process. As mentioned, all sorts of implements can be utilized for the production of excellent patterns. The main things to keep in mind are the character of the molding, the texture necessary to harmonize with the picture and what the final finish is to be. Experiment in producing textures with sponges, cloth and other articles.

Textures can also be achieved by painting the frame with several rather heavy coats of casein paint and then scraping it when dry with a special tool or with sandpaper. The same rules apply as for wet texturing except that it is more difficult to correct errors. However, the effects which result are worth the work entailed.

First give the frame several coats of casein and sand smooth. Take a piece of coarse (No. 2) sandpaper and using a straight, even stroke, cut the area to be textured with fine, irregular lines. When this type of texturing is finished, particularly with glazing, the depressions hold the color and the stain is wiped off the high spots which then appear lighter in tone.

As a second exercise, scratch the frame as before, but cross the scratches at right angles with long, even strokes along the length of the molding. This type of texture is only successful on very plain Moldings having large flat or curved surfaces.

As a final suggestion, use scraps of glass for the first attempts with texturing and try out every implement that may occur to one. The smooth surface of the glass makes it easy to draw the tool across and shows up the pattern readily.

While scratched and combed textures may be only faintly apparent when working with the solid color casein paint, the final treatment will bring them out boldly, so do not be apprehensive if the work appears rather flat and uninteresting at first. Texturing is not an end in itself and only has importance in regard to the final effect. *Glazing, Staining* or *Shading:*

This process has all of the above names but the one which seems most accurate in meaning is "glazing", or the spreading of a thin coat of dark color over a lighter, painted surface. It has great value in frame finishing because of its flexibility and because it can be used to produce smooth, softly-toned effects, stipples or wood-grains. The last named is not to be confused with literal copying of the grain of woods, but merely to give an over-all feeling of natural wood in any color desired.

For practical purposes, a pint or so of a neutral-color glazing mixture should always be kept on hand. Raw umber in place of black should be used for the basic mixture. Since every picture requires individual treatment, it is usually necessary to make a special mixture for each job. Therefore, pure colors can be blended with the neutral glazing base to tone it slightly one way or the other. Like the methods used for texturing with casein paint, glazing solutions should dry slowly enough for working properly. Do not worry about too slow a drying quality, although too much linseed oil is to be avoided. To insure hard drying in twelve hours, it is a better plan to have the undercoat sufficiently non-absorbent rather than to add linseed oil.

Glazing mixtures are composed of oil color which usually contains some white to dull the color and a mixture of three parts of glazing liquid (sold under the name of flatting oil) to one part of turpentine with linseed oil added only in the amount necessary to slow down the drying. Once mixed, it keeps quite well but must be stirred very thoroughly before using. Glazes will appear very much darker than may be desired for the final value, but wiping or graining will make them lighter.

First experiments in using glazing for finishing frames should consist of wiping with a soft cloth pad. Coat the frame evenly with the glazing mixture and let it set for a few minutes. Now fold a piece of soft cloth (like cheesecloth) into a pad and wiping along the length of frame with a light, even pressure, remove some of the thin paint. Repeat giving even lighter pressure than before until the frame is smoothly toned all over. Practice this method on scrap pieces which have been first given a good ground coat of white oil paint sanded smooth. By leaving a heavier glaze in depressions or corners, it is easy to impart an antique feeling to the frame.

On another prepared piece of scrap try the graining method of glazing. For this a 2" FEATHER-TIP GRAINING brush will be needed. This is a thin, wide brush with flexible, but not soft, bristles. Goat the frame as before and allow it to set. Take the graining brush and with a long, steady stroke "brush" the frame, lifting it up only when the stroke has been completed. Now "brush" the frame in the other direction and continue back and forth until it has reached the value desired.

Remember that the general coloring of a frame should not be too strong. While any color can be used for glazing, always add more white than pure color to the mixture. If it should so happen that too dark or strong a finish has been given to a frame, it can be remedied by rubbing very lightly with fine steel wool. This will show more of the white undercoating to make the frame lighter in value.

Without trying to imitate the natural grain of different woods, a handsome appearing finish, resembling rare wood, is easy to achieve by the use of subtle color in the glazing mixtures. Dull yellow browns with a greenish cast or mixtures with a trace of purple give the feeling of rare, tropical woods.

After the glaze has dried thoroughly, touches of color or gold can be rubbed on the decorations or the edges of Moldings to relieve the plainness of the finish.

If a frame has been textured with casein paint and a glaze finish over it is desirable, it will be necessary

69

to size the casein paint with a thin white oil paint or with pure white shellac so that it will not be too absorbent. Undercoats for glaze finishes require a hard, smooth surface. To achieve this quality, add ¼ pint of gloss white to every pint of flat white oil paint plus a few drops of Japan drier. *Rubbed Color:*

One of the most useful processes in finishing *is* that of rubbing accents of color or gold over flat areas, on high spots of ornaments and decorations or on the edges of frames. Any oil color can be used as well as gold compo xx (which is gold bronze paste in a tube) or aluminum paste.

To rub color, take a small piece of cloth and place it over the index finger, pulling it down snugly and holding the ends in the palm of the hand. Pick up a small amount of oil color on the tip of the covered finger and work it into the cloth by rubbing on a piece of newspaper. Now, with a very light touch, rub it over the parts of the frame which are to be accented. Rub extremely lightly at first and gradually increase the pressure until the effect desired is obtained. Charge the cloth with color as often as necessary, always rubbing away the excess on newspaper to get the right value. The most useful color for this purpose is burnt sienna. Its warm, reddish-brown tone seems to harmonize well with most water color or oil paintings. When applying the color, do not attempt to make it too even because it should only be used to break up the plainness of the surface and add interest. Nor should one saturate the cloth too heavily with color, because this will make the color too dark and strong on the frame. The effect to be aimed at is one of color coming through the finish rather than of being applied on top.

Even without decoration, ornaments or texture to pull the color from the cloth, this method of rubbing on color can be used on flat surfaces, particularly the narrow top edges of certain Moldings. A pleasing, softly-rubbed appearance rather than a hard, solid line is obtained.

Gold Compo XX paste or aluminum paste can also be employed with very good results to highlight ornaments. It dries in about an hour and needs no burnishing. They are rubbed on also but not in the same fashion. The bare finger is used, since the metals to be applied should give a much more solid effect than that of a color. The value of gold compo in finishing picture frames cannot be stressed too highly as the following will show.

Many attempts are made by inexperienced beginners to achieve an "antique" appearance on ornamented gold frames. They are not usually successful except by accident because the method used tries to bring the gold or ground color through the basic coat after the frame has been completely covered with paint of one sort or another. The perishable quality of the gilding is rarely taken into account and is usually rubbed away when some of the paint is removed, thus exposing nothing but the composition base of the ornaments. With the use of color and gold compo as described, the frame is merely cleaned, given a basic finish and then the color and gold accents are added, by disregarding the original finish, much time is saved and good results assured.

Spattering:

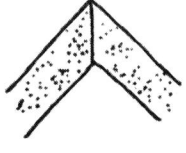

This *is* one of the most helpful operations in finishing frames. Since the drops of paint appear to merge together at a short distance, they have the function of pulling the unevenness of the finish or the touches of color and gold into a unified whole. Spattering can be done by using a piece of wire screening and a toothbrush, or by using a small pencil brush (artist's water color brush) and tapping it on a stick after it is charged with paint. The drops of paint thrown by the latter method are less regular than those made by the wire screen and toothbrush. Furthermore, the drops can be controlled from very fine to heavy and directed almost exactly on the area to be covered.

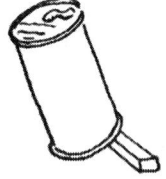

While spattering can be done with any color, it is wise to use the neutral color of raw umber for the first trials. Because spattering is an operation which does not take long but which will be used very often, it is advisable only to mix enough for each job at a time. For the purpose, it will be found handiest to use the bottoms of empty tin cans by turning them over, although any small receptacle will do that can be wiped clean with waste when the work is finished. Place it in a slanting position and put about ¼teaspoon of raw umber oil color near the highest part and pour turpentine into the lower.

Using a pencil brush, mix only enough to charge the brush. Hold a stick in the left hand about six inches away from a piece of white paper and tap the ferrule of the brush against it with a gentle, light motion. Always make a sample of the spatter after

72

charging the brush with paint. Observe the density or the size of the individual drops. If the effect is too faint, try tapping the brush closer to the paper. If it is still too light, the brush needs more paint. Try it again and if the drops are then too heavy or large, remove some of the paint from the brush by stroking it once on a piece of newspaper. The process may sound involved, but with a little practice it is easy to make the brush hold exactly the right amount of paint to get the correct spatter. *Basic Finishes:*

The following pages deal with specific basic finishes which have been tried and proven successful. They are not to be followed rigidly. *Natural and Stain Finishes:*

Moldings used for natural or stained wood finishes must be of clear wood free from knots or sap streaks (light and dark areas). The wood will have to be well sanded and brushed very clean to remove all traces of dust.

All that is necessary for a medium gloss, natural wood finish is to give the frame one or two coats of clear white shellac. When dry, rub it down with fine steel wool and wax carefully with a good grade of paste wax.

For the occasional frame to be stained in one of the popular finishes such as oak, walnut, mahogany, etc., it is advisable to buy small quantities of penetrating stain in those shades. However, for quantity production a range of water-soluble stain powders are preferable. Once mixed, they can be intermixed to produce any shade or color desired. Because water-

73

stains raise the grain of the wood, it may be necessary to sand the frame lightly again before applying finishing coats of shellac and wax. After the stain finish is dry, proceed as for natural wood frames.

A high gloss finish, while rarely desirable, may be called for at certain times. Give the frame a coat of shellac to seal the wood. After rubbing lightly with steel wool, carefully apply a coat of spar varnish. When it has dried overnight, rub it down with wet-or-dry sandpaper, using water or oil. Then give it a finishing coat of wax.

Natural or stained wood frames are sometimes enhanced by having an edge or some part of the molding painted with a color to repeat some note in the picture. A stripe or an edge in gold is also effective.

Natural *finish:*

1. Sand very smooth
2. One or two coats white shellac
3. Steel wool
4. Wax

Stained finish:

1. Sand very smooth
2. Stain
3. White shellac
4. Steel wool
5. Wax

Pickled Wood

This finish is easy to apply and can be of great variety in color while maintaining the feeling and appearance of natural wood. Properly applied, the finish will harmonize with any type of contemporary picture and interior. One rule only is to be observed, keep the washes as nearly white as possible. Use pure white casein in a thin solution on all but the very darkest woods. Pickled wood finishes are exceptionally durable and will not soil easily.

The frame should be made of carefully selected molding in order to have an attractive grain. After careful sanding, scratch the frame with long, even strokes along its length using No. 1½ or No. 2 sandpaper. Be sure to avoid crossing the scratched lines diagonally or at right angles because the scratches will show up strongly after the wash is applied. Try not to go over the scratches more than once or the grain will tend to be obliterated. Raw oak molding does not need scratching.

First stain the frame with the desired color of wood stain and when dry coat it with clear white shellac. When the shellac has dried, rub down very lightly with fine steel wool. Give the entire frame a thin wash of white casein paint and when this has dried, rub down to expose the stained wood. The casein will remain in the scratches and the softer parts of the molding. Wax and polish for durability.

Stained Finish:
1. Sand smooth
2. Scratch with sandpaper.
3. Stain
4. Coat of white shellac
5. Steel wool
6. Casein wash
7. Steel wool
8. Wax

Natural Finish:
1. Sand smooth
2. Scratch with sandpaper.
3. Casein wash (white)
4. Steel wool
5. Wax

Glaze-Stained Wood

This is another natural type wood finish, except that the staining is done with the neutral mixture used for glazing over painted surfaces. It dries with a pleasing grayish tone resembling driftwood.

Sand the frame smoothly and coat with the neutral glazing mixture. Allow it to set and wipe off enough to expose the grain of wood. Add color to the mixture for special tones. Wax lightly and polish.
1. Sand smooth
2. Coat of glazing mixture
3. Wipe
4. Wax

Combination *Textured and Plain Finish*

First texture the inside of the frame with a straight cross stroke using a wide-toothed steel comb. Paint the frame solidly with dark, Venetian red oil paint and when dry, paint on touches of blue, green and yellow in swatches at random. After drying, give the entire frame a thin wash of neutral casein. When dry, rub with steel wool to expose the color and some of the ground coat slightly. Only rub the part which has been textured. Paint the plain outside edge with burnishing gold and burnish.

This finish will have a neutral appearance but is enlivened subtly by the color showing through.

1. Texture inside of frame
2. Coat with Venetian red oil paint
3. Paint swatches of color at random
4. Coat with neutral casein
5. Steel wool inside
6. Burnishing gold outside
7. Burnish

Two-Tone or *Two-Color Finish*

Two-tone finishes are particularly effective on frames having sharp divisions in the profile or which have only a part of the molding textured. Only two suggestions are offered herewith because the variations are endless and the beginner is urged to attempt his own combinations. Besides the two tones or colors used on a frame, in certain instances it will look well to paint the top or inside edge with a contrasting color or with gold.

Texture the frame on the inside only with a diagonal stroke. Coat the frame with white oil paint or white shellac. When dry, glaze the inside, textured area with a dark, warm brown and wipe off to expose the high spots of the texture. Glaze the outside of the frame with a light, neutral tone and grain with the graining brush, keeping the strokes running along the length of the frame. Accent with rubbed color or gold compo along the top or inside edges.

An entirely different effect can be given to the same frame by glazing the inside with a very light off-white glaze. Then paint the top and outside solidly with some color to harmonize with the picture.

1. Texture inside of frame
2. Coat of white oil paint or white shellac

3. Glaze inside with dark brown or
   Glaze inside with off-white
4. Glaze outside with neutral mixture or
   Paint top and outside edge with solid color
5. Rub color or gold on top edge

Neutral Casein Finish

This particular finish will be found to harmonize with the majority of pictures. It is easily applied and is a good time saver.

Coat the frame solidly with white casein and when dry sand down smoothly with 1/0 or 2/0 sandpaper. Paint the frame with a coat of white oil paint (for use over calsomine) or with white shellac. When dry, apply a very thin wash of neutral color casein. Sand very lightly with 3/0 sandpaper barely enough to show the white undercoat in an uneven fashion. Be careful not to cut through to the bare wood, especially on sharp edges and high spots. Rub touches of color on with a cloth wrapped over the finger. Avoid having too much color and be sure not to make it too even. Variation gives vitality to the finish. Apply touches of gold compo or aluminum paste, being sure to cover the edges or parts which catch the light. Spatter the frame with raw umber or another color.

1. Sand
2. Coat of casein
3. Sand
4. Coat of white oil paint or white shellac
5. Thin wash of neutral casein
6. Rubbed color
7. Touches of gold or silver
8. Spatter

"Antique-ing"

It may be desirable occasionally to make a frame look as "antique" or ancient as possible. Besides giving it an antique finish, the molding itself can be artificially aged.

First, all sharp edges and corners are rounded unevenly with files and sandpaper in order to make them look worn from handling. Ornaments are softened and made less distinct in form in the same way. Next, irregular patterns of tiny holes to imitate worm holes are produced by jabbing the plain parts of the molding with a scriber, an ice-pick or similar implement. All parts of the molding are also to be marred and made uneven by cutting and denting. Scratch deep lines, unevenly spaced, at right angles to the grain with a knife or other sharp tool in order to represent checks. Whatever will make the frame worn or old looking is to be used. On solid wooden Moldings, a short length of heavy chain struck at random will make interesting marks. The frame is then ready to receive any number of "antique" finishes. Antique *Finish No. 1*

Paint the frame with one or two coats of casein paint tinted to a light, warm gray. Rub colors into all parts of the frame, skipping the deepest depressions. Then rub raw umber over the entire frame, then yellow ochre followed by touches of chrome yellow, Venetian red, burnt sienna, etc., until the entire frame is covered. The brighter colors should be used sparingly and keep all colors uneven.

Make a thin solution of burnt sienna and turpentine and paint it lightly and irregularly over most of

79

the frame. Avoid too solid an effect. Now highlight the edges and ornaments with gold compo and spatter heavily.

1. Two coats warm neutral casein
2. Rub on plenty of colors
3. Irregular wash of burnt sienna and turpentine
4. Gold compo
5. Heavy spatter

Antique *Finish* No. 2

This finish will be found excellent for use with heavily-ornamented, second-hand frames since it will be found easy to apply and will produce an over-all soft effect, thus minimizing the distraction of heavy ornamentation.

Clean the frame, disregarding the original finish. Paint the frame with white casein paint followed by one coat of white oil paint for use over kalsomine. In place of the white casein, the frame can be given two coats of white oil paint. When dry, coat the frame with a thin wash of neutral casein. Using a rather wet cloth, remove a considerable amount of the wash, particularly from the edges, beading, ornaments, etc. Rub touches of color on sparingly and irregularly. Apply gold compo in the same way, making it blend into the color. Spatter heavily.

1. Clean frame
2. White casein
3. White oil paint
4. Wash of neutral casein
5. Wipe off
6. Rub on touches of color

80

7. Rub on gold compo
8. Spatter heavily

Antique *Finish* No. 3

The general effect of this finish is that of metal leaf although it is produced entirely through the use of paints. It is extremely useful and can be easily varied by using a differently colored undercoat, aluminum bronze instead of gold or by giving the final wash coat a definite color tone. It can be made to harmonize with any picture very easily and is time-saving.

Give the frame two coats of Venetian red oil color containing japan drier. When thoroughly dry, paint the frame with high quality bronze paint. After drying, rub the frame lightly and carefully with fine steel wool until the red undercoat begins to show through on the edges and ornaments. Dust the frame and give it one coat of clear white shellac. Next paint it with a very thin wash of neutral casein and after it dries, wipe off the edges and high spots with a wet cloth and then spatter lightly.

1. Two coats Venetian red oil paint
2. Coat of gold bronze
3. Rub down with fine steel wool
4. Thin coat of white shellac
5. Wash coat of neutral casein
6. Wipe off
7. Spatter lightly

Bronzing

Metallic powders in various shades of gold, aluminum or in colors mixed with a binding medium are called bronze paints and their application is called "bronzing". In order to overcome the "radiator paint" effect which most bronze paints give, the finish is usually glazed with oil color or with a wash of casein. The process is convenient for rapid finishing, and properly handled will give handsome results.

Sand the molding very smooth and coat the frame with white shellac. Rub down with steel wool and then apply one or two coats of the bronze paint. When dry, coat with white or orange shellac. Next *give* the frame a coat of an oil glazing mixture and wipe off the high areas with a cloth. A thin wash of neutral casein, followed by wiping with a damp cloth, can be used instead if desired.

1. Sand very smoothly
2. Shellac
3. Steel wool
4. One or two coats of bronze paint
5. White or orange shellac
6. Glaze with oil glazing mixture or
   Wash of neutral casein
7. Wipe off highlights
8. Spatter if desired

(Another method of bronzing giving a smoother finish is as follows: Coat the frame with gold size and allow it to become almost dry. Place the bronze powder on a piece of glass or waxed paper, and taking a folded pad of very soft cloth dip it into the powder. Now tap the charged pad lightly on the frame until it is completely covered with bronze. Shake off excess powder, shellac and proceed as above.) Burnishing

Burnished gold will give a soft, glowing, metallic

finish which is excellent for entire frames, inserts, headings, etc. After the burnishing solution has dried, it is polished with a smooth agate burnisher. Some burnishes are made of glass, but agate gives a better polish. On irregular surfaces or decorations, the burnisher hits only the higher places, leaving a matt effect in the depressions, thus making a pleasant contrast.

BURNISHER

Only burnish bronze powders can be used for burnishing; other bronze powders merely darken when rubbed. It will also be necessary to make the following stock solution for mixing with the powder. *Stock Solution:*

Take about one ounce of rabbit skin glue, cover with water and soak overnight. Add about one cup of water and heat in a double boiler until the glue is completely dissolved. This is the stock solution and will thicken when cool, but it will regain a fluid state on re-heating. For use with the burnish powder, dilute with water in the proportions of one part of stock solution to three parts of water. The result is called GLUE SIZE.

To mix the burnish powder for painting, dissolve about *Yi* ounce of the powder in two tablespoons of alcohol and then add about ¼cup or one ounce of the glue size. Experiment with slightly different proportions until a mixture with good covering strength is achieved.

In order to have the burnishing mixture adhere properly to the surface to be burnished, it is necessary that a water-base finish first be applied to the molding. Use either clear glue size or casein paint.

83

Burnish gold will be found exceptionally useful for touching up minor damage on gilt frames.

Sand the frame smoothly and apply one coat of either clear glue size or casein paint. When dry, sand very lightly with 3/0 sandpaper. Coat the frame with the burnish gold mixture. Be sure to flow it on, otherwise it will be streaky and the brush will pick it up when overlapping. If two coats are necessary, allow the first to dry thoroughly for an hour or more. Rub beeswax on a soft cloth and wipe the frame lightly with it. Burnish with an agate or glass burnisher, rubbing back and forth with short strokes until the entire surface that can be touched by the burnisher has been polished.

1. Sand very smoothly
2. Coat of glue size or casein paint
3. One or two coats burnish gold mixture
4. Beeswax
5. Burnish

Gilding

Because gilding requires experience and a good deal of proficiency to produce successful results, it is one of the phases of frame-making which is a profession in itself. Most of the larger commercial frame shops employ finishers whose only work is the laying of leaf. Its use in picture framing is becoming more and more restricted, however, in favor of the softer, more adaptable and neutral, painted finishes.

Occasionally, part of a molding such as an inside edge, beading or a decoration will look exceptionally well when gilded with metal leaf instead of being bronzed or burnished. Metal leaf provides a crisper accent than the other two methods described.

Even with the gilding restricted to only one part of a frame, many frame shops now purchase their moldings pre-finished and merely cut them to size. It is debatable whether the amount of time spent in gilding is repaid. The largest frame houses, with the passing of heavily ornamented frames, now mostly do their gilding with quick-drying gold size (adhesive for the leaf) and with metal leaf. Metal leaf is a substitute for the more expensive and difficult to handle genuine gold leaf which requires an ultra-smooth surface and a room absolutely free from drafts. Metal leaf is easily protected from tarnishing with a thin coat of shellac.

Because of the difficulty in manipulation and the great expense, it would be extremely unwise for the beginner or the occasional frame maker to attempt gilding with genuine gold leaf. Numerous books exist on the entire subject of gilding and repetition here of so highly specialized a subject would be superfluous. A description of a quick method of gilding with metal or aluminum leaf (genuine silver leaf is also rarely used today), however, will be in order.

Metal or aluminum leaf is comparatively easy to apply because it is much thicker than real gold leaf and therefore will not fly around at the slightest breath. All leafing requires a smooth surface to be successful. While genuine gold leaf needs at least two coats of glue size and two coats of gilders clay size, frames for metal leafing can be prepared quickly by merely coating the smooth molding with two coats of shellac and rubbing it down with fine steel wool. If it is desired to have some color such as Venetian red or black show through the gold to imitate the clay size used for real gold leaf, it can be accomplished by first painting the frame with oil paint. After it has dried, it is shellacked and rubbed down as before. Gold size to hold the leaf is then applied in a thin, even coat and allowed to become almost dry. It should have a slightly tacky quality, and the fast-drying gold size will be ready for gilding about two hours after application. Be sure to cover every part of the area to be gilded with a solid coat of the size, otherwise the frame will be bare of leaf in spots. The temperature of the room must never be allowed to become too low while gilding and must be free from dust and draughts. Do not attempt to apply the leaf while the size is too wet or it will wrinkle and bunch up.

Assuming that the size has dried to the right degree, the frame is now ready for the application of the leaf. All leaf is packed in sheets of 25 to the pack called a "book". Metal and aluminum leaf is considerably larger in size than either the genuine gold or silver and is therefore doubly economical. At times, it may be easier to have the frame lie flat and at others it may be necessary to rest it in a slanting position against a stand of some sort. Now open the book of leaf carefully. It will be found that each leaf is separated by a piece of tissue paper.

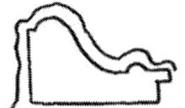

Pick up the book with the thumbs on top and the index fingers beneath. Starting with the outside edge of the frame, bend the book forward and over the molding until the leaf covers the frame. Use the index fingers to press the leaf firmly to the frame. Now, with

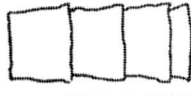

OVERLAP EACH LEAF

86

a soft, bristle brush or with clean cotton, tamp the leaf down into the carvings or depressions. Allow the next leaf to overlap the first generously and proceed to cover the entire frame. There are bound to be bare spots or breaks. They should be covered immediately with scrap leaf and also tamped down. When the gilding has been completed, the frame will present a ragged appearance due to the over-lapping. Excess leaf can be removed in several ways; by simply rubbing it gently with cotton or by using a soft clothes brush which has been rubbed with beeswax. Always be careful to rub *with* the laps and not against them. Professional gilders use a brush called a "tip" for picking up the individual leaves and "leading" them into position. It is first rubbed over the palm of the hand or the hair a few times to pick up the merest trace of oil. The oil makes the leaf adhere lightly to the tip. The tip is also used for pressing the leaf down into the depressions of the molding.

AFTER GILDING — BEFORE CLEANING

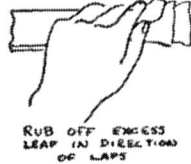

RUB OFF EXCESS LEAF IN DIRECTION OF LAPS

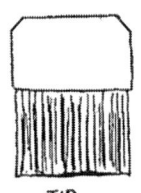

TIP

"LEADING"

1. Sand very smoothly
2. Two coats of shellac
3. 3. Steel wool
4. One coat of fast-drying gold size (Any type of gold size can be made to dry faster by adding a few drops of Japan drier.)
5. Allow size to dry to the point where tackiness is barely perceptible and then gild frame with metal or aluminum leaf as described
6. Shellac metal leaf with white and aluminum leaf with orange shellac
7. Glaze with oil glaze or coat with wash of casein
8. Wipe off
9. Light spatter if desired

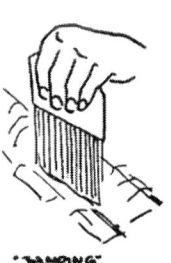

"LEADING"

87

CHAPTER EIGHT

DECORATIONS

REFERENCE HAS BEEN MADE concerning the decoration of frames by using the seven basic motifs of design alone or in combination as outlined in the book A *Method* for *Creative Design* by Adolfo Best-Maugard.

It is the purpose of this section to point the way toward the simple decoration of frames so that the beginner can exercise his own ingenuity and taste. It would be only too easy to present a set of patterns and rigid formulas to be used for the decoration and finishing of picture frames. The beginner in frame-making will do well to learn first how to finish frames so that they harmonize with the pictures and only later consider the problem of carved decoration.

When a simple, straight cut is added to a curved surface, an entirely new form is created. If the cut is repeated over and over, a pattern is achieved. When a simple, half-round beading is given a cut repeated at regular intervals, a continuous interesting line, rich in itself, is formed. Cut the lines at an angle and the line becomes animated; moving all around the frame. This type of decoration serves to break up the hard lines of the frame and help it to blend more easily with the picture. If the theory of decorating only a ridge or an edge is applied and if the frame is carefully finished, the result will be quiet, harmonious and tasteful.

Carving decorations of any size on the corners alone can never be anything but distracting since they tend to pull the observers' eyes away from the picture itself. Exactly the opposite is achieved by using a simple, running, geometric motif. In fact, the decoration can be emphasized subtly by picking out the high points in color or gold or otherwise accenting it. It might be pointed out that a certain school of picture framing insists on carved corners and then, after gilding, makes every attempt to break up the effect of the carving by rubbing the metal leaf through in spots to the ground underneath. If distinct carving must be done, it should at the very least be of a continuous pattern and in addition minimized by a soft, neutral finish.

Certain motifs will suggest themselves readily to the framer for use with particular pictures. Combinations of a simple curved line of some kind together with another shape of line used in texturing the ground can be so integrated that any effect desired can be produced. The spirit of the painting can be easily extended into the frame.

The following suggestions are merely indications to help the beginner get started on one of the most interesting phases of frame-making; one of the first so far in this book that will challenge his taste, ingenuity and perception of what is needed to make each frame harmonize perfectly with its picture.

If there are not enough scraps at hand left from cutting miters and joining the frames, or if frames have been purchased ready-made, the beginner should secure several pieces of scrap wood of various lengths and thicknesses. A commercial frame shop may be a source for scrap pieces of actual picture Moldings, although this is doubtful because of all craftsmen, framers seem to be the most parsimonious. . . . At any rate, the edges of the scraps should be rounded or planed to different angles in order to have varying shapes with which to experiment.

Small ridges or the edges of Moldings should receive small cuts close together and the larger parts should be worked with heavier tools. The wood rasps, an occasional gouge and perhaps a triangular shaped piece of metal are all that will be needed for the start. The triangular shaped piece may be an old nail set ground or filed to a point along one side as shown.

Take a small, rounded edge of scrap and make cuts first with the triangle rasp and then with the round one at half-inch intervals. To keep the esthetic quality throughout a frame, it is usually advisable to make the cuts round or square in relation to the type of molding being decorated. Employ a round file for beading or curved surfaces and a triangle rasp for flat or angular planes. At any rate, practice making cuts the same depth at regular intervals until a certain degree of uniformity is reached. First make the cuts at right angles and then diagonally. Now try marking the center of a piece of scrap and make diagonal cuts radiating from each side of the center. Curved lines are best left to the texture, although they can be done by using a small gouge. The straight or diagonal cuts can be spaced further apart and a round dot punched with a prick-punch for variety. A prick-punch is used for marking metal.

ENLARGED
END OF NAIL SET

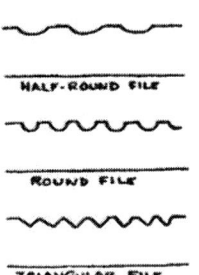

HALF-ROUND FILE

ROUND FILE

TRIANGULAR FILE

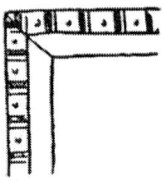

The small triangular shaped implement mentioned previously can be used to decorate small headings by holding it in the left hand and tapping lightly with a hammer. Be careful not to make the dent so deep that it breaks the grain.

Edges of large Moldings can be given a shallow, wavy line by filing with the half-round rasp.

On wider, heavier ridges it may be necessary to make shallow saw cuts at the proper spaces before the actual filing or gouging is done. If the lines are to go in different directions from the centers, it is advisable to make a template as a guide for drawing the lines in pencil before cutting. Take a piece of cardboard or stencil paper and mark a straight center line with directional lines at an angle from one side. Cut them through the board neatly as shown. When using it, first find the center of each piece of the frame to be cut and mark the lines all along one side to the miter. When nearing the miter, try to space the lines so that they come out quite evenly. Reverse the card, find the center and mark the other side of the molding. Repeat for all four sides. With a small back saw, cut into the lines to a depth of about $\frac{1}{8}$". The triangle rasp or the round one can now be used to complete the cut. Be sure to sand down the decorated parts so that the sharp edges are removed.

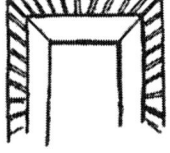

TEMPLATE

These simple, geometric decorations can of course be added to the painted finish while it is being textured. Circles and curved lines are particularly effective when made in this way. The rigidity of filed or carved lines is avoided which helps to soften the entire frame.

91

Another effective and easy method of adding decoration to simple frames is through the use of ready-made decorative Moldings such as beading, rope, etc. They can be purchased in a large variety of sizes and widths and are easily attached to the Moldings with brads and glue.

Frames decorated with these Moldings are particularly effective if the finish is not too heavily textured and if the molding is accented by rubbing with touches of color or gold. These ready-made Moldings will add richness to the frame and give it just as much an harmonious result as hand-carved decorations.

CHAPTER NINE

REPAIRING DAMAGES

WHEN A FRAME needs extensive repairing or touching up, it is usually both quicker and more satisfactory to refinish it completely after repairs have been made. Minor repairs, however, can be made successfully without too much effort and without re-finishing the entire frame.

Artists sending pictures to exhibitions have definite problems because the frames rarely return in the same condition in which they were sent. Packing, unpacking and repacking, handling while hanging, etc., all leave their tell-tale marks. The artist is lucky if the joining of the corners holds, let alone the finish. If the frame has a durable surface, only a cleaning and perhaps minor touching up is necessary. It is therefore a wise course to apply a finish which either does not show handling or is readily re-finished. Casein paint finishes are comparatively fragile but are the easiest of all to re-finish. A good plan might be to decide on a basic finish and to use it for all pictures sent to exhibitions.

For this purpose, a standard for mixing neutral basic tones should be made which should be adhered to at all times. Finishes can then be duplicated quickly and with a minimum of effort. For example, as a basic neutral finish for casein paint, one can decide to use three parts of white casein and one part of raw

93

umber. Once the proportions have been decided, a reasonable amount should always be kept on hand.

Through accident, a frame is sometimes dropped or struck, causing a dent, knocking off some of the decoration or otherwise injuring it. If the damage is not severe and the joints have not been loosened, it is usually sufficient to repair the damaged spots with crack filler and merely touch them up. If the damage consists of a dent, so that the finish is pressed into the wood but still adheres, it will be necessary to remove the finish before filling the depression. Scrape it away carefully with a knife and scratch or otherwise roughen the dent to hold the crack filler. Make a mixture of filler rather on the thin side and apply it carefully, using a small spatula to smooth it off level with the surrounding wood. It may be necessary occasionally to size the filler after it has dried and been sanded before touching up with either water colors or oil paints. This repair cannot be made successfully to finishes which have been evenly toned by glazing, but may be used on any finish that has irregularity of color or surface.

For smooth surfaces, it is more efficient and satisfactory to use "Repair Sticks". These are available in all colors and all shades of gold and silver. They are simply rubbed or melted with a match into the depression and polished with a cloth until level. They are similar to shellac sticks but consist of some type of wax and coloring matter.

Should a small piece of the frame be knocked or split off, it is important that the area be roughened and that small tacks, nails or brads be driven in to

act as armatures when the crack filler is applied. For practice, cut or damage a piece of scrap molding and try various kinds of repairs.

When an old frame with fragile, plaster ornaments is badly damaged, it is sometimes possible to salvage it by knocking off all the same type of ornaments (the beading, for instance) around the frame. It should then be sanded with rough sandpaper and simple decorations substituted if necessary. This method will only work if a uniform effect can be achieved. The work involved is wasted if the frame is in such poor condition that so many ornaments have to be removed that the frame is practically bare. Try to estimate the time needed to repair the frame and always examine the frame carefully to see whether it is worth the work that may be involved. *Casting Ornaments For Repairing*

First oil the ornament or section to be duplicated. Soften red dental *impression compound* in very hot water and work it out to a sheet 1/8″ or more thick and large enough to cover the section so that about 1″ extends all around. Saturate a cloth with hot water, and working the compound until it is soft and pliable by repeated dippings in the hot water, quickly press it down over the ornament, using enough pressure to make sure that it is forced into all the- crevices. Use the wet, heated cloth while pressing down if the depressions are very deep. Allow it to cool and harden and then lift it off carefully. The mould is now ready for casting, but first oil it lightly and then construct cardboard supports so that it will not tip over when the plaster or compound is poured in. Adjust the sup-

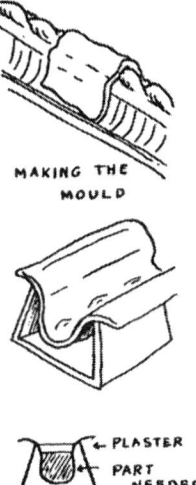

MAKING THE MOULD

← PLASTER PART NEEDED

ports so that there will be a more or less flat surface where it is most needed. Mix the plaster of pans to the consistency of very thick cream and ladle it into the mould, jarring occasionally to force out air bubbles.

After the plaster has set completely, but before it is completely dry, remove from the mould. It may be necessary to dip the entire assembly into hot water to soften the compound. This should be done so that it literally "falls away" from the casting. Because the casting is not yet hard, handle it very carefully. Place it face down and see how much of the back of the casting needs to be carved and sanded away before it will fit snugly into place. Begin the fitting process and proceed very slowly and carefully. After repeated trying and cutting, the section will fit perfectly. Allow it to dry thoroughly and then coat both the ornament and the space with glue. Attach the casting and bind it with string or weight it down until the glue is dry. Flow very thin crack filler into the remaining cracks or spaces. The frame is now ready for re-finishing but before doing so, remove all traces of oil or grease with the proper solvents.

CHAPTER TEN

MATS AND MAT-CUTTING

Mats, as distinguished from mounts, are flat pieces of cardboard or other material that have an opening or "window" cut in them to reveal that part of a picture it is wished to show and to help in isolating it from a background. They may be in any color, plain, decorated or covered with some material such as cloth or paper.

It will be readily seen that a small or delicate picture, whether a print or a drawing or a water-color, needs something as an aid to vision. Wide mats do not necessarily dwarf a small picture. On the contrary, hanging on the wall, such a mat would certainly draw the eye more quickly to the picture than if it were framed close. Arbitrary sizes for print mats exist and it is unfortunately necessary to observe them when matting or framing prints or drawings, etc., for exhibitions. However, when a print or water-color is to be matted for framing to take its place as a decoration, certain sound practices should be observed, always bearing in mind that some pictures require distinctive treatment. White or off-white mats are most commonly used and will be found suitable for most of the pictures which need matting. At other times, a lightly tinted mat or a "French" mat, that is, one with decorative lines of different kinds around the window, will make a tremendous difference in the final appearance.

Again, a mat covered with paper of a certain color or quality, or a textile will be effective. Or an especially thick mat may be in order. First, however, it is necessary to discuss mat-cutting technique.

Sense of proportion must be exercised for good matting. Until enough experience has been gained, the following rule should be observed. Always make the bottom of a mat slightly wider than the top and sides. This is necessary in order to compensate for an optical illusion which makes the bottom of mats having all sides equal appear narrower. The eye normally travels from top to bottom and must have more area for rest at that point. In the case of rigid, standard mat sizes, it may not always be possible to have the bottom wider than the sides, but it must *always* be wider than the top even if only slightly.

When matting fine prints such as etchings, lithographs, etc., it is advisable to cut the window large enough to reveal the plate mark. This is the slight depression caused by pressure when the etching or other print is made. Another reason is because prints of this type are usually signed by the artist outside the actual printed area and it is desirable to show the signature.

The first requisite for mat-cutting is a good knife. As mentioned in the list of essential tools, paper dulls a cutting edge quicker than any other material. Therefore, the knife should be thin and of high quality steel to take and hold an edge as long as possible. Remember that it is easier to sharpen the knife than it is to cut a new mat over again because one side may have been spoiled by a ragged edge. Standard knives for

mat-cutting are made but they may have to be ground down before they are really suitable.

Next to the knife in importance is a good straightedge. Mats will never be satisfactorily cut without one. If possible, a metal straightedge long enough to handle the largest sized mats to be cut should be procured. One edge should be beveled because either beveled or straight-cut mats can be made with it. Lacking the metal kind, secure a good quality, metal-edged and beveled wooden ruler as long in length as necessary.

The third requirement is to have a fresh surface under the mat board for every cut to be made. This will help to eliminate ragged edges and slipping. Scrap pieces of smooth cardboard are suitable and a sufficient number should always be kept on hand for the purpose.

To prevent the metal or wooden straightedge from slipping while cutting, adhere one or more strips of scotch masking tape to the bottom. Felt or sandpaper, if not too thick and cemented to the bottom, will also provide the necessary friction. The straightedge should be kept clean at all times. It is wise to hang it up when not in use to avoid damage or contact with paint or grease.

Pumice stone of the finest grade, art gum and a blower or a draftsman's brush should also be on hand for cleaning the mats.

The average picture, both in content and size, will look best in a mat which is about 3" wide at the top and sides and 3½" *on* the bottom. The term "about" is used because it sometimes occurs that ¼" one way

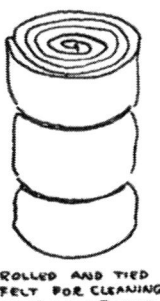

ROLLED AND TIED
FELT FOR CLEANING
MATS WITH PUMICE

or another will not harm the finished appearance and may result in considerable savings over a period of time in mat board, backing and glass. For instance, by planning to use the dimension of at least one side of standard picture glass sizes, a saving in cutting time and lessening of breakage when cutting is made. In addition, there is certainly a great deal less possibility of error when cutting Moldings if one uses the larger fractions of inches in measurement. Contrast the ease of marking and cutting a piece 16" compared to one 15⅞". Such slight differences in mat sizes are not noticeable, provided good proportion follows throughout.

Taking for the first problem a picture requiring a mat 3" wide at the top and sides and 3½" wide on the bottom, horizontal in shape, and the area to be visible measuring 12" x 14". Add the width of the two sides (6") to the length and the total of the top and bottom (6½") to the shorter dimension. The outside measurements of the mat will then be 18½" x 20". Trim a piece of mat board to this size, making sure that the corners are square. Next, using a pencil compass set at 3", draw lines for the top and sides by letting the pointed end slide along the edge of the mat board as shown. Re-set the compass to 3½" and draw the bottom line. Be careful not to let the lines extend too far beyond the area to be cut out.

There are two schools of mat-cutting: Cutting from the face or top of the mat board or cutting from the back. Greater care in marking and cutting needs to be exercised if mats are cut from the face but on the other hand, it is easier to make sharper edges. The straightedge must be placed at least 14" from the line and the knife drawn firmly and steadily along it, always holding it at the same angle. If the mat is marked for cutting from the back, the straightedge must be placed directly on the line and the cut made as before but with the angle reversed. The exact window size is more likely to be achieved with this method, although the front edges may not be as sharp. As in joining frames, finishing and everything else connected with the craft, it is advisable to experiment with mat-cutting using scrap pieces of mat board. First try making clean, vertical cuts and then increase the bevel. Try seeing how sharp a corner can be made. In connection with this, it will be found that after the four sides of a window are cut, the center may still adhere slightly at the corners. Slip a double-edged razor blade through the cut and complete it at the corners with the same angle as the bevel.

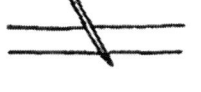

Mats are to be judged by the cleanness of the cut and the even quality of the bevel. It is a skill which an unfortunately few number of artists or home craftsmen possess. It is not difficult, but requires care and with a little practice, mats of professional quality can be produced.

When cutting mats, lay the board on a level surface with a piece of scrap cardboard directly underneath the line to be cut. This line should always be near the front edge of the bench. Holding the straightedge firmly down with the left hand, start the cut boldly and draw the knife slowly and evenly to the corner.

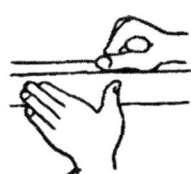

French Mats

CORNER- FRENCH MAT

As described, French mats are ones with decorative lines drawn around the window. These may consist of a plain double line in black or color or may be combinations of lines and bands of color or gold painted on. At the height of the popularity of French mats, women were employed who did nothing but paint in the delicate water-color washes. This style of mat still has its uses and can add interest to a drawing, water-color or color print. Its use with black and white prints appears to detract from the picture. French mats are relatively easy to make and only require care so that the lines do not overlap at the corners. To avoid this, very faint pencil lines should first be drawn in as guides and later covered with ink or paint. If one plans to use a band of color to be edged with lines, paint the color in carefully and then draw the edging lines with a ruling pen. For old prints, use a sepia or brown ink and faded looking colors. When a real antique-faking job is to be done, first select a cream or off-white mat board for the mat. Make a wash of a light, cool brown water color and paint irregular areas on the mat with it, particularly near the edges. When a section has been painted, allow it to set for a minute or so and then blot it up lightly with clean blotting paper. Next, make another wash, perhaps a slightly stronger gray and spatter the mat unevenly. Keep all the colors very light in value so that they merely look like discolorations of the mat board itself. This process is suggested if it is necessary to replace a genuine antique mat which has been damaged.

SHADED AREAS: LIGHT BROWN

102

Still another decoration which is of value both when used alone and in combination with French mats, is that of painting the bevel of the mat in gold or color to harmonize with a particular tone in the picture. Always work from the back of the mat, holding it up at a convenient angle. Use a ¼" or ½" wide long-bristled, flat brush, keeping it flat against the bevel and drawing it at an angle from the front of the mat to the back. Do not attempt to paint with the tip of the brush, and never allow the brush to slide off completely since this will force paint on to the face of the mat. Also, do not charge the brush with too much paint. It is better not to try to paint too great a length of the bevel at once, but to use short even strokes.

A tinted or colored mat will be in order for some pictures. The mat can be either painted the right tone or covered with paper or a textile. In spite of the fact that the mat and bevel are to be covered, care is still needed in the cutting because irregularities will show through. Lay the paper or textile face down on a smooth, clean surface. In size, the paper should be at least an inch larger all around than the mat. Coat the mat board with a proper adhesive such as paste and place it carefully in position. Cut out the center area (which is to be discarded) about one inch smaller than the actual window size. With a sharp knife, make four cuts running from the exact corners of the window to the inside corner of the paper. Next coat the back of the mat solidly about one inch in from the window edge and smooth the paper over carefully. Proceed with all four sides of the window

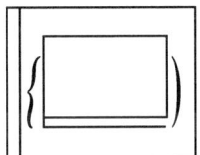

and then do the same to the parts extending beyond the outside edges. Care and extreme cleanliness are needed to make a neat mat using this method. Always try a sample of the paper or fabric on a piece of scrap board first.

An alternative method of covering mats is to cut the window to the proper size in the regular way, then cut the mat into four parts by drawing lines from the corners of the window to the outside corners. Mark or number adjacent sides so that the corners can be reassembled properly. Each piece is then covered separately, later gluing the four pieces down in position to the board of the mounted picture.

Mats for pictures already mounted should be glued down to the picture and the mounting board to prevent unattractive space from appearing after the picture is framed. Brush the glue or paste thinly up to about I/4" of the edge to be seen through the window. Place the mat carefully in position and dry under pressure for an hour or two. Trim the excess mounting board which projects beyond the edges of the mat.

Ground pumice stone or art gum will be found most useful for cleaning mats. The pumice removes a very thin portion of the paper and carries with it paint, glue and other foreign matter.

Unless exceptionally wide Moldings are used, it is always advisable to mat small pictures.

CHAPTER ELEVEN

MOUNTING *PICTURES*

MOUNTING, as differentiated from matting, means the adhering of a picture to a backing. It is extensively used whenever the operation will not destroy any of the intrinsic value of the picture. For example, all prints which have a plate mark showing or those which are hand-printed such as wood-cuts or engravings would lose in value if they were mounted. However, water-colors or sketches and paintings on paper as well as drawings can be mounted and will be the better for it because they will not buckle after framing. If an artist is framing his own pictures, he can use his discretion whether or not a picture should be mounted. If the framing is being done for another person, however, it is advisable to obtain permission before proceeding and particularly if the picture is a valuable original. Mounting is also used for reproductions of all kinds, maps and pictures on perishable paper which are to be preserved. A special board with a very smooth surface is manufactured for mounting, but any good cardboard, beaver board or pressed wood can be used.

Photographs and some other pictures are usually mounted on board before framing rather than with window mats. The mounting board forms the mat or background. Special care must be used in this case so that none of the adhesive is squeezed from under

105

the picture on to the mat. In addition, the picture must be placed in the exact position on the mounting board. To eliminate the latter problem, mount the picture on a considerably larger board and trim it down later. As a matter of fact, it is better to mount all pictures on boards larger than the finished size, even those to be matted.

Oil paintings on canvas may sometimes need mounting on a piece of fresh canvas and then re-stretching. If the canvas is fragile, but the layer of paint is in good condition, this is an admirable way to preserve it from damage. Dents or tears in canvases are automatically removed in this way.

There are many adhesives (also called "moun-tants") and many ways of mounting. All of them are more or less satisfactory, but it is wise to select that method which gives the least warping when dry. Whatever method is employed for mounting, extreme care should always be used to avoid getting any of the adhesive on the face of the picture. Warping is caused by the gradual shrinking while drying of the paper or fabric which has been moistened. The more the moisture content is reduced while mounting, the less warping will be encountered. Adhesives

The familiar rubber cement, as is well known, will adhere paper to board smoothly and with a minimum of effort. However, because of its tendency to dry out in a relatively short time, it will lose its holding power. It may also discolor the picture mounted with it through chemical action. Its use must be completely avoided except for the temporary mounting of charts and pictures of no real value.

Good quality library paste will be found useful for certain types of mounting work, especially small pictures. It must be spread very smoothly and the work must be put under sufficient pressure until dry.

Mounting which appears to give the smoothest adherence is called wet mounting. Different adhesives can be used for this method, but the principle is that the picture to be mounted is dampened enough to lose its stiffness and its tendency to curl. It will stretch in size when wet, but while drying under pressure it will shrink and all air bubbles, wrinkles, etc., are removed. Wet-mounting usually requires the use of a process called counter-mounting, that is, the adhering of a sheet of paper to the *back* of the board before it is put under pressure or otherwise dried. The paper used for counter-mounting, drying at the same time as the picture, tends to neutralize the pull or warping of the board. The mounting of large reproductions is usually accomplished by this method. Warping can be reduced to a minimum, but never completely eliminated by counter-mounting.

Another method of mounting, used chiefly for photographs, is called dry-mounting. It involves the use of a very thin sheet of dry mounting tissue placed between the picture and the board. Heat is then applied and the picture is permanently mounted.

The newest, and what appears to be the best method of mounting large pictures (paper) on board employs a synthetic latex compound. A coat of the compound is given the mounting support, the picture is carefully laid upon it and then rolled down from

107

the center outward to press out all air bubbles. After pressure of medium weight for an hour or so, the mounting is finished. Warping is very slight and the mounted work does not acquire that "stiff as a board" quality but retains a certain flexibility. This factor helps greatly in reducing the frame-twisting tendency —which wet mounting has.

Mounting canvases which have been removed from their stretchers requires a rather different technique. Before coating the back of the canvas with hot glue or synthetic resin glue, it is first roughened with sandpaper. It is then laid carefully on a piece of fresh, unsized linen which has been ironed smooth. The canvas is adhered by rolling and is placed under heavy, even pressure long enough to insure thorough drying. Tears or holes should be covered with waxed paper to prevent the pressing boards from sticking if any glue is forced through.

Valuable pictures and those on thin paper should only be mounted on illustration board or other white stock of high quality. Impurities in cheap pulp board may strike out through and discolor the mounted work. All mounting board should be smooth and comparatively free from imperfections. Pictures to be framed under glass need not be mounted on very heavy board, since the pressure of the backing board in the frame will hold them flat against the glass. Those to be framed without glass require heavy board or what is referred to as 2- or 3-ply mounting board. Pressed wood, beaver board and other process boards can be used to good purpose, particularly for extra large pictures.

The use of wheat or wall-paper paste for mounting has largely been superseded by newer adhesives on the market. Wheat paste is economical, easy to mix and use but it has the bad fault of attracting attack by mold or vermin.

If mounting is to be a regular part of one's framing work, certain basic equipment is needed. The most important item is a heavy hand roller such as those used for rolling down linoleum. It can be either of the single or double roller type, the latter perhaps being a bit easier to handle and giving greater pressure while rolling.

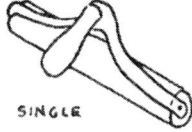

SINGLE

A table high and large enough to lay out the mounting board and the picture to be mounted at the same time is also necessary. It should have a smooth clean surface. To prevent the adhesive being accidentally spilled on the surface, cover the table with paper while mounting.

DOUBLE

Push-pins will be very useful to have on hand for mounting. They are to be used for pinning down the picture so that it will remain flat while moistening or applying adhesive.

A press or an area large enough to lay the mounted work down evenly should be available. Extra boards or sheets of plywood should always be at hand to place over the work before weights are added.

Brushes and suitable receptacles for glues, etc., are all that remain to be added to the equipment.

NOTE: Before putting any mounted picture under pressure, make absolutely sure that the surface of the picture is free from adhesive. Wipe up excess paste around the edges also.

Rubber Cement Method

Lay the picture to be mounted on the mounting board and mark its outline. Next, place the picture face down on newspaper and using a stiff brush, coat its back evenly with the cement. Brush the area marked on the mounting board evenly. Allow both surfaces to dry completely and holding the picture by the corners, allow it to drop on the board. Press down with the roller and remove any excess cement by rubbing with the fingers until it is loosened.

Library *Paste Method*

Mark the position roughly on the mounting board and lay the picture face down on newspaper. Place push-pins in each corner and give the back of the picture a smooth coat of paste. Lifting it by the corners, carefully place it on the mounting board immediately. Cover with clean paper and roll down, then lift the covering paper off, wipe up excess paste with a damp cloth and place under medium pressure until dry. Wheat or WaJl-Paper Paste *Method*

First prepare a thin solution of ordinary wall-paper, paste or use a mixture of casein paste according to the directions on the container.

Mark the position of the picture on the mounting board and lay the picture face down, securing the corners with push-pins to prevent curling. With a very wet cloth or sponge moisten the back of the picture until it is limp and lies quite flat.

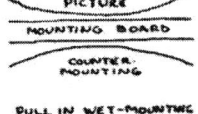

Using a wide bristle brush, spread a smooth, thin coat of paste on the board and also the back of the picture. Make sure there are no bristles from the brush, lumps of paste or other foreign matter on either

110

pasted surface because they will show as bumps very distinctly after the work has dried.

Remove the pins, and lifting the paper carefully by two corners, lead it into place starting with the free end. Before rolling it down make sure that it is in position and reasonably smooth. Then, working from the center toward each edge, roll it down firmly, wiping up excess paste squeezed out by the roller. Do not be alarmed if bubbles persist or if it does not appear to stick properly in places. They will disappear as the picture shrinks while drying.

Turn the picture face down on a clean surface and cut a piece of wrapping or backing paper larger than the board. Brush a generous coat of paste on the mounting board covering it completely and then wet the paper thoroughly with a cloth or sponge. It is not necessary to apply paste to the paper. Lay it down on the board, and lifting one end, smooth it from the center outwards as before. Use a large, clean cloth or a regular, wide wall-paper hanger's brush. Do not attempt to smooth too large a surface at once and try to make it as even as possible. Turn the picture over again and trim off the excess counter-mounting paper with a razor blade.

Place the mounted work under heavy pressure, using either a press or several sheets of cardboard and heavy weights. It should not be removed until about 24 hours later.

The great drawback to this method is the amount of time consumed in counter-mounting and drying. It is partially offset, however, by the excellent work turned out. All wrinkles and buckles are erased while

111

drying and it is practically foolproof because it dries so slowly the picture can be shifted or moved while mounting if necessary. Dry-Mounting *Method*

Mounting with dry-mounting tissue gives superb results. It is quick, clean and foolproof but unfortunately requires a large press with thermostatically controlled heat to make the tissue adhere properly. Because of the necessity of a press (which are only made in limited sizes), it is impractical for the framer to attempt using it. An occasional small picture or photograph may be mounted by this method using an electric iron, but considerable experimentation is necessary to discover the correct temperature. Too much heat will melt the tissue and too little will keep it from sticking. Caution must also be taken not to damage delicate colors with the heat. Unless a press can be purchased and much mounting of photographs is done, it had better be avoided altogether. *Synthetic Latex Compound Method*

Mounting with these compounds is actually mounting with rubber cement, but with this difference: the mounting is done while the latex is in a fluid state and contact with air causes it to change chemically and practically weld the picture to the board. After this change takes place, no ordinary solvent of any kind including lacquer thinner will affect it. Once mounted, the picture can never be removed. While the compound is in its milky-white state it can be diluted with water.

Mark the position of the picture on the board and brush an even coat of the adhesive on, keeping the strokes straight across the board first one way and then crossing them. Work rather quickly with plenty of latex because the board may absorb some.

As soon as the board has been covered satisfactorily, lay the picture down carefully and lightly. Do not attempt to shift it once it has touched the adhesive nor try to smooth it down by hand. Starting at the center, roll it down firmly toward each edge. Then roll the entire picture, first in one direction and then across, using heavy pressure. Avoid getting any of the adhesive on the roller or the face of the picture.

Place the picture under medium pressure for an hour or so and the mounting is then complete.

If any bubbles occur which seem impossible to remove with the roller, place the picture under heavy pressure for two hours or more. Wrinkles where the picture may have been kinked or folded can be removed while mounting by placing a piece of clean paper over them and rubbing or "ironing" them down with a bone paper folder, a very smooth knife handle or similar implement.

A word of caution: Do not attempt to mount thin papers with this method.

The brush should be washed out immediately with soap and warm water or it can never be used again. Mounting *Canvases*

Remove the canvas from its stretcher carefully and place it face down on a clean surface, smoothing out the edges which have been bent. Secure the corners with push-pins and roughen the back slightly with No. ½ sandpaper.

Stretch a piece of pure, unsized linen (which

113

should be larger all around than the canvas to be mounted) on another smooth surface, using pushpins around the edges.

Moisten the back of the canvas with a damp cloth and coat it with thin, hot glue. Lift immediately and lay it down carefully on the linen. Place a sheet of clean paper over the face of the canvas and roll it down from the center outwards using heavy pressure.

Lay waxed paper on several sheets of cardboard if you are not using a press and place the mounted canvas back down. Now place more waxed paper on the face of the picture, add more cardboard, and then weights. It will be dry enough for re-stretching in four to six hours. Finishing Mounted Pictures

Sprayed lacquer is of course the most efficient and desirable method to use for coating mounted work, but because spraying equipment is not usually owned by the average home craftsman, it will not be considered in this section.

Brushing lacquer is very difficult to handle and should be avoided completely. Its quick drying properties make a smooth finish virtually impossible except for very small pictures.

Occasionally, mounted pictures such as good-sized photographic enlargements, reproductions of original works, maps and so forth, are framed without glass. It is therefore necessary to protect them from soiling by giving them a coat of varnish and/or wax.

In place of lacquer, mastic picture varnish will be found most suitable. Because of the varying rates of absorption of printed and painted surfaces, it is advisible to size the surface to be finished with a glue size. LePage's glue, diluted with water to a very thin, watery consistency will serve well.

Always use a good varnish brush and flow the size or varnish on in order to reduce brush marks to a minimum. Sizing and varnishing should only be done in a dust-free room of even and not too low temperature.

Photographs need not be varnished but can be protected by waxing with paste wax and then polishing.

115

CHAPTER TWELVE

PASSE-PARTOUT

A VERY USEFUL, though more or less limited and temporary method of framing a picture is by the use of passe-partout, or binding the edges with paper or cloth. It is especially well suited to small pictures and will last a considerable time if correctly applied.

In order to produce the best possible binding job, it is essential that all of the component parts be cut to exactly the same size. The backing, the mat if one is used and the glass must be carefully cut to exact measurements. Another important feature is that the tape must have just the right degree of moisture when it is applied. Too much will wash the glue away and too little

CUT ALL TO EXACTLY THE SAME SIZE

will not permit it to adhere properly. Paper tape in colors, made especially for this work, is available at any good stationer's. However, ordinary brown gummed tape is just as suitable and it can be painted easily to match any color scheme. The same applies to gummed linen tape, although the additional cost is not warranted for this work.

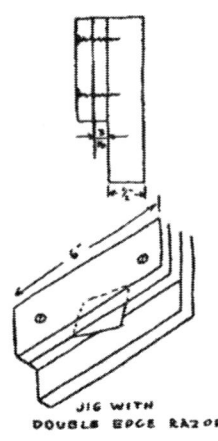

The successful passe-partout job calls for evenness in the tape which shows on the front of the picture. This can be achieved by first pasting the tape into position and then trimming it off evenly later. A razor blade held in the small holder illustrated will make exactly the same margins all around.

JIG WITH DOUBLE EDGE RAZOR

Assuming that the picture is assembled and ready

for binding, first insert a ring for hanging through the backing board. Now secure any two opposite sides temporarily with scotch tape to prevent slipping. Cut a strip of the tape to be used for binding about one inch longer than the side to be bound. Moisten a piece of cloth or a small sponge in a weak glue-water solution. Wet the tape and holding it by the ends, place it along the edge, allowing about 3/8″ to extend over the face. Fold down the edge over the glass and smoothing it carefully along the edges, fold the lower part over the backing. Using the trimming jig, carefully cut along the edge and lift off the waste. Repeat with the opposite side. Remove the scotch tape and proceed to bind the two remaining sides. This type of finishing is very useful for inexpensive, small pictures used as decorative notes or for reference.

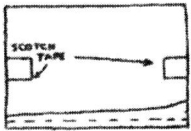

TRIM ON DOTTED LINE

TRIM SHADED PORTION

Passe-partout is also used to bind sheets of original manuscript, letters, paper printed on both sides, etc., between sheets of glass to protect them while handling for reference or study. Other uses will readily be found for the method.

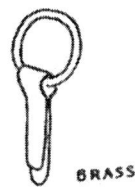

BRASS

Occasionally passe-partout can be combined with a heavy, thick, wooden mat and glass to make an attractive frame. The fact that it may not last as long as a regular frame is offset by the low cost of materials and the speed with which it may be accomplished.

LINEN

Passe-partout may be applied when framing antique costume, flower or bird prints with attractive results. The work is enhanced even more by using pastel-colored mats, plain or French, or by painting a black mat with a gold line directly on the inside of the glass.

117

CHAPTER THIRTEEN

CUTTING *GLASS*

THE PRIMARY REQUIREMENT for accurate glass cutting is a smooth, clean working surface. It must be smooth because any irregularities may cause breakage through uneven pressure when cutting. It must be clean so that the glass will not be scratched if it is shifted. Flaws in the glass such as air bubbles are bad enough but scratches show up as black lines if a light mat is used. As suggested in the section on assembling, a large, sturdy bench is essential which can be covered with heavy wrapping paper or sheets of cardboard kept aside for the purpose. The cardboard can be used over and over again.

A good straightedge of the non-beveled kind will be found necessary. Scotch tape attached to the underside will help prevent slipping and extra precautions must be taken against this happening. Because glass has such a smooth surface, it may be necessary at times to drive brads into the surface of the bench to keep the straightedge in the proper place.

A glass-cutter as described in the list of tools is all that remains necessary. Glass-cutters with diamond points last forever, but their extremely high cost make them only practicable to those whose trade is glass-cutting.

The cutting of glass is not difficult and the relative cheapness of the material allows beginners to break a few pieces. Even the artist who works only with oils and does his own framing may be called upon occasionally to frame one of his black and white sketches under glass, so for anyone doing framing, glass-cutting should be learned. It is interesting to compare the price of a piece of glass cut to size and purchased in a retail store with the small cost of doing it oneself.

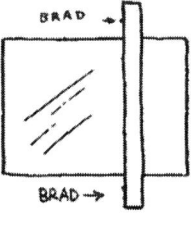

Brush the surface intended to be used for glass-cutting clean before laying the glass down and measuring. After it is in position, place the straightedge down in approximately the right place. Now drive two brads long enough to project above the straightedge so that it will not slide towards the left as the cutter is drawn along its right side. Taking an accurate ruler, place it on the straightedge at right angles and extending towards the left. The wheel on the glass cutter is slightly less than ⅛" from the bearing surface of the cutter. This difference must be taken into account when measuring. For instance, if a piece of glass were to be cut to exactly 20", the measurement from the right hand edge of the straightedge to the left hand edge of the glass would be slightly more than 19⅞".

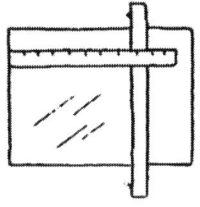

After sliding the glass under the straightedge, measure the top and bottom to see that they are equal, then grasp the cutter in the right hand like a pencil placing the index or middle finger in the curved part provided for it. Holding the cutter at a slant and starting as close to the furthest edge but never beyond it, draw the cutter towards yourself giving it firm, even pressure and letting it slide off the nearest edge. An even, scratching sound will be heard and if it has been correctly done, the glass will be "started" in the

same way that a piece of ice or a diamond is split.

Lifting the glass carefully by the largest part, tap gently at either end of the cut with the handle of the cutter. Tap on the under side of the glass opposite to the cut and only at the beginning or the end of the cut. The glass will be seen to split. The waste area can now be grasped and by bending slightly, parted.

Practice on scrap pieces of glass, making the line as straight as possible. Try different pressures until one has become accustomed to the correct amount and also to the degree of slant. It requires a trick or a knack but it can be learned by anyone in ten minutes.

Never go over a line once cut and never cross a cut line. It will only dull the cutter and break the glass. It is better to discard the glass and save the cutter.

Cutting oval or irregular shapes is not difficult but merely requires a steady hand since they are cut freehand. Lay the glass over a pattern and follow the line. Leading lines, curving away from the cuts are then made and the pieces broken off in sections.

The glass cutter should always be kept in turpentine. This is not only to protect it from rust, but because the slight, oily film makes for smoother cutting. Generous amounts of oil should be left on the cutter when cutting very old or extra thick glass. Glass gets brittle with age.

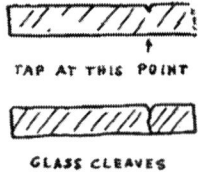

TAP AT THIS POINT

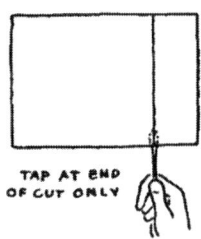

GLASS CLEAVES

TAP AT END
OF CUT ONLY

BREAK OFF SECTIONS
BY TAPPING END OF
CUTS.

120

CHAPTER FOURTEEN

ASSEMBLING

ASSEMBLING (or fitting) is the final operation of fastening the picture in the finished frame, applying the backing paper and attaching the hanging material. This part of picture framing also requires the utmost cleanliness and careful workmanship. A badly assembled picture, no matter how carefully the component parts may have been executed will present a sloppy appearance in a short time. It will admit dust, become loose in the frame and eventually "go to pieces". On the other hand, a well-assembled picture will actually reinforce the frame and maintain its fine appearance for many years.

Cleanliness of the working space and freedom from dust will be found to be of considerable aid when assembling. A sturdy work bench with an area twice the size of the largest pictures ordinarily framed will be found necessary. It should have a smooth surface so that if it is also used for glass-cutting, an even contact can be made and thus help eliminate breakage. Sheets of heavy cardboard, cut to fit the top, should be kept for use when assembling if the bench has a rough surface. If the bench is smooth, heavy wrapping paper will be sufficient covering.

A small amount of additional equipment will be required for assembling. Battens, a small scraper, a hammer with at least one flat side and perhaps a "fit-

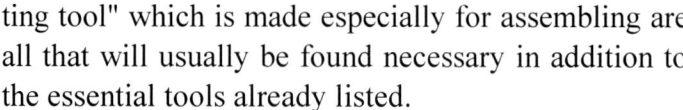

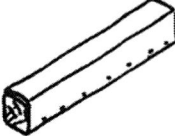

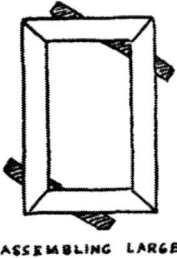

ASSEMBLING LARGE
PICTURES

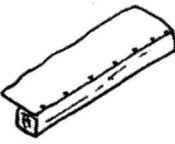

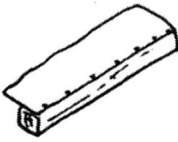

COTTON PADDING

ting tool" which is made especially for assembling are all that will usually be found necessary in addition to the essential tools already listed.

BATTENS are felt-covered strips of wood used to avoid damage when laying the picture face down while assembling, backing or attaching hanging material. Almost any kind of wood can be used, but it should be thick enough so that frames with projecting ornaments will not come in contact with the bench top.

2" x 2" fir, left as it is but with two edges rounded with a plane, will be excellent. Two 36" pieces are usually long enough for assembling average size pictures. Should both dimensions of a picture be larger than 36", the battens can be placed at an angle across the corners.

After the edges have been rounded, cut two strips of felt 5" to 6" wide and 36" long. Tack one side of a strip along the edge of each batten as shown. Now lay cotton padding or several carefully folded thicknesses of soft cloth along the entire length and stretching the felt over it, tack it down on the other side and trim off any excess. Left uncovered, the bottoms will not slide around and yet the battens will not be so heavy that they cannot be shifted readily. Because even gritty dust can injure a delicate finish such as metal leaf, it is important that the battens be used every time a finished frame is to be placed face down.

The HAMMER for driving brads when fastening should be a small, light tack hammer with the left side (looking at the face) ground flat as shown. Flat-

122

sided hammers called tinner's SETTING OR PANE-ING HAMMERS are ideal for the purpose. An eight or twelve ounce hammer should be heavy enough for all assembling work.

The FITTING TOOL will be found efficient and indispensable if a considerable amount of assembling is to be done. Its cost *is* not great and will be quickly repaid through time saved. It is particularly valuable when fitting pictures into narrow Moldings because it can be adjusted to force the brads to exactly the depth required for holding and so avoid driving them completely through the frame. With the tool, the shortest brads can be forced in to a specified depth for the narrowest molding as well as fitting pictures into Moldings up to 3 or 4 inches wide.

A small SCRAPER, obtainable in the 5 and 10c stores, will be needed for cleaning out the rabbet before inserting the picture.

Besides the above tools, the DRAFTSMAN'S BRUSH (used for cleaning mats) and the PLIERS (already purchased) will be needed ready at hand. The pliers may be used for forcing in the brads and will be found necessary for removing temporary nails or those bent when hammering.

Before any assembling is done, it is absolutely imperative that the rabbet of the frame be perfectly flat and clean. There should be no heavy drops of paint or glue remaining because they will interfere with a good contact between the picture and the frame. When glass *is* used, even a tiny drop of paint or glue may be sufficient to break *it* and even if that luckily does not happen, a space will be left which will admit

123

dust Be sure to clean the rabbet with a small cabinet scraper or a knife blade and then brush the frame clean.

The number-size and length of brad needed for good assembling varies, of course, for each picture but certain safe rules to follow might be that more brads are required if the frame is large and finer brads are needed if the molding is narrow. For the average size picture and molding, brads driven in 2" apart will be enough for secure holding.

Assuming that the glass has been cut to the correct size and carefully cleaned and the matted picture with the backing board ready, lay the frame face down on the two felt-covered battens. The battens should be close enough together to allow the narrow part of the frame to extend over them an inch or so. Now, making absolutely sure that there is no dust or foreign matter between the glass and the mat or picture, lift the assembly and lower it carefully into the frame. Another method of placing the picture in the frame is to lay the assembly of glass, picture and backing board face up on the battens and then to place the frame over it. Holding the thumbs on the front of the frame and the fingers on the backboard, turn it over by swinging the edge furthest away toward one.

It is good procedure to drive one or more nails temporarily in each side and to turn the picture over for final inspection before fastening permanently. Check whether the area shown is correct (if the rabbet measure is considerably larger than the sight measure) and whether the window of the mat is parallel with the frame on all sides. The sides of the mat

124

should also be equal; they can be checked easily by using a ruler. First measure the top and bottom of a side and then compare it with its opposite. If any shifting is necessary, it can be done by inserting a knife blade in the back to force the assembly one way or another without removing the nails. Turn the picture face up again and re-check before proceeding. Inspection takes little effort at this stage compared to forging ahead and then having to remove many nails to correct the job.

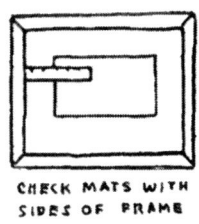

CHECK MATS WITH SIDES OF FRAME

If the picture is now satisfactory, the following method should be employed for permanent fastening. At least one brad should be driven in each side to hold the picture exactly where desired before removing the temporary nails. The advantage of the following manner of driving brads is that the picture will be held as tightly as possible against the lip of the rabbet and shifting cannot occur later.

Hold the brad with the left hand at a slight angle and tap it lightly to drive it partially into the backing board. Caution should be observed so that the brad does not penetrate too deeply. It should be started about one-half to two-thirds of its length in distance from the molding. Now, pressing it down while tapping lightly, force it through the backing board and into the molding to the depth necessary for secure holding.

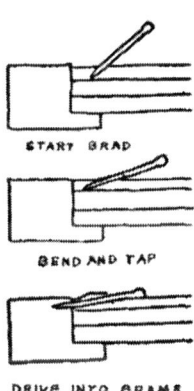

START BRAD

BEND AND TAP

DRIVE INTO FRAME

Proceed to drive brads along the entire length of one side, either the one nearest or towards the left.

The same method of inserting the nails at an angle through the backing board should be followed when using the fitting tool. It may be necessary, however,

125

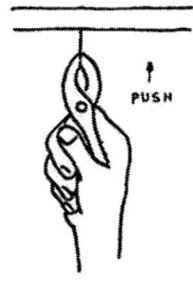

to start the nails with a hammer and then finish forcing the brad into the wood with the previously adjusted tool. A tiny circle of felt, cemented to the stationary leather buffer, will help protect fine finishes.

As mentioned, the pliers can also be used to force brads into the molding and there may be times when this will be the only possible way. The nail is grasped by the pliers near the head and forced through the backing board into the molding at an angle as before. When using the pliers, it will be found most convenient to drive the brads into the edge of the frame farthest away.

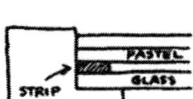

The fitting of pastels into frames requires an insert of some kind to prevent the picture from coming in contact with the glass. Pastel is the most delicate and perishable of all mediums and must always be handled with the utmost care. In spite of the fact that a pastel may have been fixed with fixatif, it will continually shed powder.

After the glass has been cut to the right size and cleaned, it is inserted in the frame. Narrow strips of wood, at least ⅛" thick, but never wider than the depth of the rabbet, are then placed completely around the inside, tacked in with fine brads and painted a dark, unobtrusive color. The inside of the glass is cleaned and brushed free of dust, the pastel and backing board carefully lowered into the frame and fastened in place. Never use a hammer, but force the brads in with pliers or a fitting tool. Hammering will loosen the pastel and cause it to shed even more.

Pictures without glass and stretched canvases require different treatment in assembling. At times, it

126

may be necessary to fasten a picture in its frame without backing board or even brads so that it can be removed easily and exchanged for another. At other times, it may be advisable to frame the picture between two pieces of glass so that both sides may be examined or so that it may be reversed for hanging. Manuscript pages are often treated in this fashion. The following method may be used if the back of the picture is to be exposed but protected.

A neatly finished appearance can be obtained by cutting four thin and narrow strips of wood to the proper length and tacking them in with fine brads. The strips and the back of the molding are then finished properly. The strips of wood should be planned to the exact thickness for holding the picture and pieces of glass tightly against the lip of the rabbet. They should be as narrow as is practical for strength. It will readily be seen that the strips will look much neater than exposed brads. There are other ways of working out this problem such as using channel frames with molding presenting the same face on both sides but since this type of work is rather rare, it need not be discussed here. At any rate, as experience is gained with regular framing work, specific problems become easier to solve.

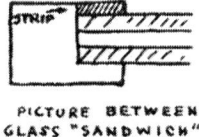

PICTURE BETWEEN
GLASS "SANDWICH"

When a frame is to be used repeatedly for the same sized picture, it can be fastened into the frame firmly but temporarily by using small, brass "turn buttons". These are available in several sizes and are attached to the back of the frame with screws of the correct size and length. The entire assembly should be of a great enough thickness so that when the button is swung

CHANNEL FRAME

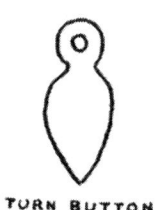

TURN BUTTON

over, it will press the whole firmly against the rabbet Sheets of paper can be added between the picture and the backing board to build it up to the proper thickness.

Assembling of stretched canvases requires a different approach. While several methods may be used for fastening, the same rules must be observed throughout. The most important one is that the canvas must never be fitted too tightly into the frame. There must always be sufficient difference between the size of the stretched canvas and the rabbet measurement to allow room for expansion or contraction. For this reason, Moldings usually employed for canvases have a sufficiently deep rabbet so that while extending over the picture, they also allow space.

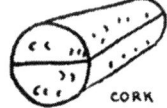

CORK

In order to prevent the canvas shifting in the frame, the space is taken up with a resilient material such as cork or corrugated board. An ordinary round cork, cut in two lengthwise, is sliced into half circles of the correct thickness, usually about ⅛". Corrugated board can be cut into strips of the proper width and used instead of cork. Any material that is at all resilient can be employed, but whatever it is, it should be fastened to the back of the rabbet with tacks or brads.

CORK
SEGMENTS

The canvas itself may be fastened into the frame by driving brads through the edges of the stretcher at an angle of 45^0 into the molding. Be careful to choose brads or small finishing nails of the proper length and weight so that the stretcher will be held but not split, and that the nails will be driven into but not through the molding.

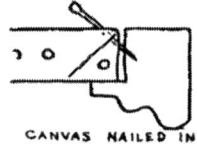

CANVAS NAILED IN

Another method is to use brass mending plates

128

bent at each end so that the screws can be driven in straight into both the stretcher and the molding. Screws can be used at both ends of the plate or at only the end fastened to the molding. If they are only fastened at one end, they can be used as turn buttons to facilitate removal or replacement of the canvas. Whichever way a canvas *is* fastened into a frame, remember that it must be occasionally removed for cleaning or re-varnishing, etc.

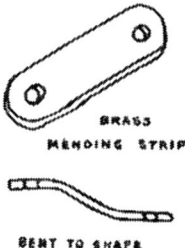

BRASS MENDING STRIP

BENT TO SHAPE

With the exception of special jobs, and pictures only temporarily fastened in frames, it will be necessary to back all framed pictures with paper to seal them against moisture and dirt. Backing paper will not only perform this necessary work, but will add greatly to the finished appearance of the job. Stretched canvases are not usually backed, except from the edge of the molding to the edge of the stretcher as shown. This is merely to finish it off and performs no useful function. A neat way of completing the framing of a canvas is to stain the *back* of the frame with walnut or mahogany oil stain.

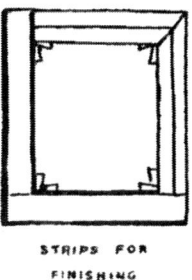

STRIPS FOR FINISHING

Successful backing is easy to accomplish and only rudimentary care is needed. The paper may be of any medium weight or color, but a dark brown or gray wrapping paper or regular black backing paper will be found to show handling less and. will therefore remain neater. Two simple practices must be observed when backing: Use only hot glue for the adhesive and always dampen the paper before applying.

The hot glue will make a permanent seal. Any simple double-boiler such as two tin cans, one smaller than the other, can be used, but a regular iron glue

129

pot will be found much more practical if any considerable amount of backing is to be done. Using a fairly stiff and narrow brush (an artist's bristle brush cut down in length is ideal) give the back of the frame an even coat. On frames wider than a half-inch or so, it is not necessary to coat the entire back, but only to paint the glue in a strip about ½" wide, starting ⅛" in from the outside edge.

The backing paper should be cut large enough to extend at least an inch all around the frame and then dampened with a cloth or sponge which is quite wet. Working quickly, but not hastily, lay the dampened side down on the back of the frame covering it completely. Smooth the paper from the centre toward each side and then to the corners, pressing it down with a clean cloth. The paper will wrinkle even more before it dries, but if the glue has been applied properly in the correct strength it will dry out absolutely smooth and taut.

The paper may be trimmed while it is still damp or after it has dried. Two methods are suggested. A small jig holding a razor blade 1/16" to 3/32" in from the outside edge of the frame may be pulled along the edge to trim off the excess. Another way is to lay a straightedge along the line to be cut (which must be determined by "feel") and then cutting with a razor blade or a sharp knife. Care must be taken in both instances so that the knife does not slip off the edge and cut the frame, thus damaging the finish. A little practice gluing paper on scrap pieces of wood and trimming along the edges is advised.

Attaching hanging material, either screw eyes or

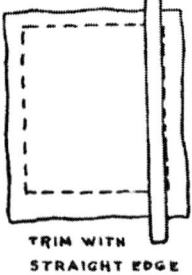

TRIM WITH
STRAIGHT EDGE

brass hangers, is the final step in picture framing. Always select screw eyes of the right size for each job. Do not use screw eyes which are too large, heavy or long for narrow Moldings nor under-sized ones for heavy frames. After points have been marked on the back for their insertion (usually one-third or one-quarter of the distance from the top edge), drill holes of the right size very carefully to a depth of about one-half the length of the screw. Care must be exercised here so that the molding is not completely penetrated. Turn in the screw eyes slowly, using a long nail or other implement and do not attempt to drive them too far. On thick Moldings of soft wood, it is not always necessary to drill a hole for the screw eye; a nail or brad awl will make a hole large enough to start the screw.

SCREW EYE

Attaching the wire is a simple operation. It should never be drawn to the point where it is taut, because unless it is long enough to form a wide V when the picture is hanging, difficulty will be experienced in keeping the picture straight on the wall. On the other hand, never make it so long that it shows above the top of the picture. Pass one end of the wire through an eye for a distance of about 2". Now bring the end back and pass it through again. Wind it tightly around the long part and repeat with the other side after making sure that the wire has been cut long enough. If the frame is especially heavy, it may sometimes be necessary to wind it around the shank of the screw eye. Try to estimate the amount of pull when the frame will be hanging and always test each screw eye carefully.

Pictures are sometimes hung on long wires from picture molding. Molding hooks will be needed and wire sufficiently long enough to reach them. The wire should be securely attached to the screw eyes and then snubbed around the molding hooks at the proper points.

Another method, particularly well-suited for framed mirrors, notices, etc., is with the use of hangers. These are attached to the top corners of the back of the frame with screws and they will cause the frame to hang flush against the wall. The hangers will be seen above the top of the frame as will the supporting hooks or nails in the wall.

BRASS HANGER

The dust proofing of pictures is a neglected part of the picture framing work of today, but perhaps rightly so when considered in the light of time spent compared to results achieved. It requires a good deal of care and necessitates scraping in order to clean the inside of the glass properly before the picture can be inserted.

Narrow strips of paper, ½" wide or less, are cut to the length of each of the four sides. They are creased along their length exactly in half. With the crease uppermost, they are brushed with paste or other adhesive and attached; one-half to the glass and one-half to the back of the rabbet. When dry, excess paste is cleaned off the glass with a razor blade and it is carefully brushed so that all dust is removed. The picture can now be inserted and fastened into place.

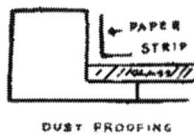

PAPER STRIP

DUST PROOFING

This method of dust proofing is not in common use today because commercial framing shops have found it uneconomical. It was originally used in Europe

132

where labor costs have always been lower. If the frame is properly made so that the rabbet is even and smooth and a good contact between glass and rabbet is made, it seems doubtful whether much additional protection is to be gained by dust proofing. It may have some uses, however, for the permanent framing of pictures for museums or other public collections.

To avoid the dust streak on walls which is so apparent after pictures have been hanging for a while, attach bumpers of rubber or cork to the two bottom corners of die back of the frame. They will serve to hold the frame away from the wall, thus preventing dust from accumulating and soiling the wall. They will also allow circulation of air and reduce attack from moisture.

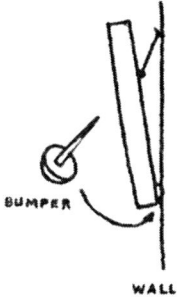

Note: Picture wire is sold by number; o, 1,2, etc., light to heavy. Make sure that wire of the proper strength is used for each picture.

CHAPTER FIFTEEN

EXPERIMENTAL FRAMES, *ORIGINAL DESIGNS*

The best of contemporary design does not attempt to break away completely from the past to create something merely for the sake of originality or newness. It attempts to utilize the best of what has gone before with the much wider range of materials available today and, in a creative spirit, to adapt the design to the needs of modern living. Louis Sullivan said "form follows function". Before we can decide on the form of the frame we must decide its function for the picture and the room in which it is to hang. It is always the first consideration of sound contemporary design in all fields. This section is therefore devoted to the integrating of pictures and their frames with furniture and living quarters of functional, modern character and not Grand Rapids "moderne".

Frames designed for pictures to be hung in contemporary interiors can and should be as sound in taste and quality as those in traditional styles for ordinary rooms. A reproduction of a picture or an original from the period of Post-Impressionism in painting to the latest school will look much more attractive in a frame of original design in keeping with the character of the picture than one based on a traditional style of molding.

The categories of Moldings designed for contemporary frames naturally adhere to the same groupings as those for traditional frames: Flat or angular, single curved and compound. However, because modem frames appear "different", confusion arises. They are merely extensions of conventional Moldings, simplified and adapted to the picture and the interior by leaving off non-functional decoration and relying solely on the "form" or profile and clean, sharp finishes for the effect.

It is lamentably true that ill-considered attempts to be different or "modern" only too often result in atrocities. With a little serious study given to the problem, however, it will be seen that contemporary design in picture framing offers many more opportunities for the artist-craftsman to show what he can create than do the traditional styles. In spite of everything, run-of-the mill styles in frames will always be re-hashes.

Experimental work in contemporary design for frames should only be undertaken by the frame-maker who has had considerable experience in all branches of the craft. It demands greater skill and a higher degree of workmanship in both joining and finishing than does the usual type of work. There are no opportunities for faking or fudging as there are when making or finishing an "antique" frame. In ordinary framing, a coat of paint covers a multitude of woodworking crimes but the joining and finishing of contemporary frames must be perfect. Imperfections are only too apparent on the smooth, clean surfaces usually employed.

CONTEMPORARY
MOULDINGS

135

When attempting the first experiments in designing original frames, it will be necessary to study die picture and the room in which it is to hang. Does the room have a quiet, restful background with muted colors and few competing pictures or are there several strong notes of color? Is the picture to take its place with others on the same wall or is it to hang alone against a large space? These questions must first be answered, because unlike conventional framing designed for characterless rooms, the frame to be created must be unique in conception and execution to play its part in making the room an esthetic entity.

If the painting or other picture is executed with powerful, pure color it may be desirable to have it "hug" the wall with a flat frame, thereby allowing the colors themselves to attract the eye. It may even be advisable to set it "into" the wall by using a shadow-box type of frame.

Unlike the suggestions made for conventional framing work, actual metal finishes, highly polished, may be exactly what is needed in certain cases. Sheet chromium, copper or brass, bent over wooden forms, may be utilized successfully alone or in combination with other materials.

Super-thick mats with straight or bevel edges; plain, textured or covered with modern fabrics and surrounded by a narrow frame may help to give a small picture the importance it deserves.

Contemporary design avails itself of modern materials and is thus truly functional. While the effort in conventional framing is centered on achieving a neutral effect, modern framing calls for the employment

136

of bold, pure color when necessary. The walls of modern interiors form perfect backgrounds for pictures and their frames.

Considering a hypothetical problem, let us assume that a picture to be framed is painted in more or less monochromatic, neutral colors. Small in size, it is to hang on a wall of soft color. First, the frame should be wide, and second, the picture should be brought forward. With these two points established, it follows that the problem can be solved easily in two ways. A wide, angle molding which would isolate the picture from the wall and bring it forward by slanting back itself could be used. On the other hand, the same effect would be achieved by framing the picture in a narrow and deep box-like frame super-imposed on a wide, flat molding.

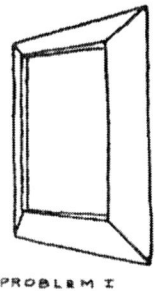

PROBLEM I
SOLUTION I

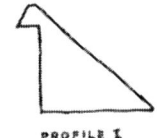

PROFILE I

If the angle molding is used, the color of the main part might be one of the lighter tones in the picture and both the inside and outside edges of the frame strong enough in color and value to form an accent and a line of demarcation.

The box-like frame mounted on a flat molding could be finished as follows: The large flat area and the outside of the narrow frame should be painted with white or off-white (or a much lighter tone of the wall color). The top edge and the outside edge of the flat part should then be painted with a deeper value of the darkest color in the picture.

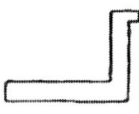

PROBLEM II

Taking as another problem; a large, brightly colored picture may need something to hold it back or to integrate it with the room which may be small and may already contain several notes of clear color in

PROFILE II

137

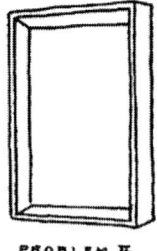

PROBLEM II
SOLUTION I

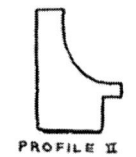

PROFILE II

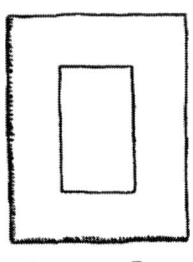

PROBLEM I
SOLUTION I

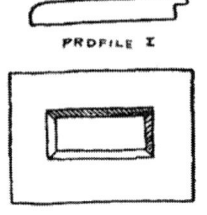

PROFILE I

SUPER-THICK MATS

upholstery or accessories. The problem now is exactly the reverse; the picture must be held down a little because it already calls enough attention to itself. One solution would be to send it back "into" the wall with a deep, narrow, shadow-box frame, perhaps one with a shallow, convex curve. A large picture of this type can take a 2" or more deep molding. If the inside edge is painted about the same color as the wall and the top or outside edges a very much darker shade of the same color, the picture will appear to retreat. Still another method of making a large, powerful picture appear smaller is to frame it with a very wide, say 6" or 8", flat frame. Perhaps the inside or outside edge could be rounded slightly. The face should be painted one or two values lighter than the wall and the outside edge slightly darker. While the over-all effect may be large, the picture itself will seem smaller.

Because some pictures require glass, do not use it merely as a protective covering but attempt to utilize it effectively in an original manner. With certain Moldings the glass can be fastened towards the front of the frame and the picture held some distance in back of it. Again, the picture could be matted in a super-thick mat and brought forward against the glass but in a very narrow, deep molding. The outside and inside edges should then be painted white or a very light color and the top edge could match the mat which in turn might duplicate some color in the picture.

Extra thick mats on pictures which need glass are usually always effective. They can be cut out of a solid piece of wallboard such as homosote, or mitered and

138

assembled out of ordinary pine. A sheet of mat board can then be glued down and a window carefully cut. The whole is painted and sanded smoothly, giving the effect of a window mat cut out of a solid block. This type of mat can be extremely effective when painted a deep, flat color if the picture is generally light in tone. If the picture is low in key, a pure white or pastel-tinted color will be best. Painting the inside edges a contrasting color provides a note of emphasis and interest. Beveling thick mats will create still another esthetic result, changing their whole character.

Contemporary framing of the type described does not aim at producing unique-ness at all costs but aims at integrating the picture with the interior in order to carry out the clean, simple lines of modern design. The picture will be emphasized in the room as it should be because extraneous, distracting pattern in the frame or the background is completely eliminated.

Simplicity, then, is the keynote of modern framing. It is not difficult to plan the width or depth, the angle or curve of a molding for a particular picture once a decision has been reached regarding the function the frame is to perform for the picture in a specific room.

The beginner's first experiments might be carried out by selecting a reproduction of a modern painting, say an abstract picture by Picasso and trying various shapes to achieve as totally different effects as possible. Design profiles of Moldings on paper according to the different purposes they should have and then try working them out with hand tools in short lengths. Place them against the picture and try to visualize how they might appear with painted finishes. If an especially good profile seems exactly right, proceed to make up the molding from plain stock or have a lumber yard do the milling if no power tools are available.

Above all, remember that modern design is here to stay and to develop; the framer with a little vision will do well to familiarize himself with it and to adapt his outlook and work to be ready for the future.

CHAPTER SIXTEEN

ADDITIONAL   NOTES

TOOLS AND EQUIPMENT

Miter *Vise*

A SMALL, efficient and inex-
pensive MITER VISE for joining frames is now available.
It will hold any average size molding securely for
fastening and is especially useful for very small frames.

Point-setter

An automatic POINT-SETTER works like a staple gun.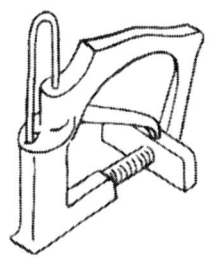
It drives diamond-shaped POINTS and makes the work
of assembling pictures quick and easy. The point is driven
half its length into the molding. The tool comes in two
sizes and its trade name is "Point-master."

When using the point-setter, back up the side of the
frame opposite the tool with a smooth wooden block to
prevent damage or loosening of the corners. Since the glass
in large pictures is heavy, the points should be reinforced at
the places where the screweyes are to be used. This will
prevent the molding from gradually being bent inward due
to the weight of the picture after hanging.

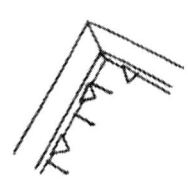

141

Plier-wrench as *Fitting Tool*

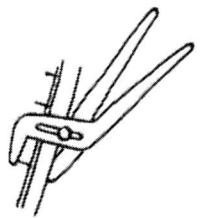

A PLIER-WRENCH can be employed as a fitting tool for driving or, rather, pushing brads into narrow frames. Pad the side of the jaw that is to be used against the molding and use the tool in the same manner as for the one described on page 17. Use care so that the brad is not driven clear through the molding.

White *Glue*

While hot glue which requires a glue pot (Page 15) is still useful for particular jobs, the plastic glue usually referred to as "White Glue" will serve well for almost all of the work performed by framers. It can be used full strength or thinned with water for mounting, gluing cloth to inserts, joining frames, etc. It is non-staining, water-resistant and dries clear and hard. In fact, it is an ideal, all-purpose adhesive for the craftsman.

INSERTS

Cloth-covered Inserts

Another method of cutting the mitered corners on cloth-covered inserts is to proceed to cover the molding as described on page 53 and after the parts have dried, lay them face down on cardboard. Now take a new, single-edged razor blade (these are available at art stores as "industrial" razor blades) and trim off the excess cloth, holding the covered molding down firmly while doing so.

142

A MITER-CHOPPER is the proper tool to use for cutting lengths of cloth-covered molding but since this piece of equipment is bulky and expensive, it would not pay to invest in it unless framing is to be done in professional quantity.

FINISHES

Quick-drying Sealer

A quick-drying, pigmented sealer with an alcohol base is available in white and in black. They can be mixed together for gray. The white dries flat and handles like an opaque shellac.

The sealer effectively covers resinous woods and colors which tend to bleed. It can be used for coating casein-painted frames prior to applying the toning color.

If raw umber pigment is added to the white sealer and it is then thinned with alcohol to a watery consistency, an excellent "graying" tone for raw wood frames will result. Give the frame a thin wash of the mixture and wipe immediately with a cloth. After it has dried, sand very lightly and wax the frame. This will attain a "driftwood" finish that harmonizes with almost any picture.

Textured Wood

Most wood used for molding can be textured in an interesting way by striating it with a coarse rasp. Hold the rasp or other scratching tool with both hands and pull it along the molding with the grain.

A heavy steel brush (like those used by butchers to

143

clean chopping blocks) can be employed to good effect. This removes the soft parts of the grain, leaving the hard parts raised. Finish with a dark stain, a neutral casein wash and then wax.

Spattering with a Spatter-Gun

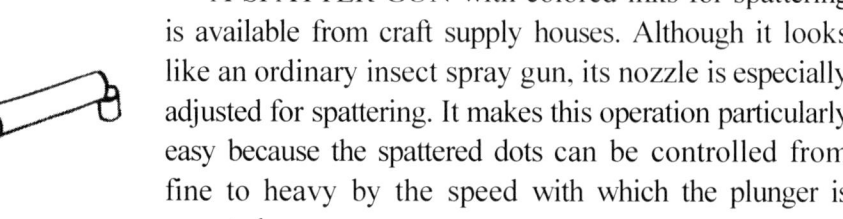

A SPATTER-GUN with colored inks for spattering is available from craft supply houses. Although it looks like an ordinary insect spray gun, its nozzle is especially adjusted for spattering. It makes this operation particularly easy because the spattered dots can be controlled from fine to heavy by the speed with which the plunger is operated.

A set of colored inks comes with the gun. Since it is not likely that any frame would be improved by spattering it with a strong color such as red, it is suggested that all of the inks be mixed together in a bottle. This will produce a neutral brownish tone that will be suitable for all spattered frames.

Gold Highlights

Gold highlights (see page 70) can be applied to edges and decorations on frames by using a brush and ready-mixed gold paint. Stir the paint thoroughly and after dipping a *Yi"* lettering brush in it, brush out some of the paint on newspaper. Hold the brush lightly and let the flat side slide along the edges of the molding and hit the high spots of the decorations. Use a light touch, lift the brush frequently and do not apply the gold too regularly.

Another method is to mix gold bronze powder with paste wax. Experiment to find the correct amount.

144

This can be applied as described for rubbing on color. (See page 70.)

MATS

Covered *Special Mats*

When a picture calls for an individualized mat, the framer may use one covered with tinted or decorative paper, or fabric, such as unbleached muslin, linen, etc. First cut the paper or cloth about 1/2" larger all around and dampen it. Coat the mat board with paste or glue and mount the material. When dry, trim off the excess with a razor.

Now mark and cut the window in the same way as for a plain mat. The bevel will be white and will make a pleasing contrast with the mounted material.

The knife must be very sharp in order not to tear the mounted material. Alternatively, the picture can be tipped on the mat, using small pieces of gummed paper as hinges or with spots of glue.

MOUNTING

Adhesive

WHITE GLUE, which is sold under a variety of trade names, is very useful for mounting. It can be used full strength for heavy materials or thinned with water for papers, etc. It dries a little more rapidly than wallpaper paste but, on the other hand, does not require as long a pressure time.

145

Canvases on Hardboard

1. Coat the *(⅛" thick)* hardboard with thinned white glue. If it dries before the canvas is mounted, it will not matter.

2. Dampen the back of the canvas with a moist sponge.

3. Coat the back of the canvas with full strength white glue.

4. Smooth down with a roller or cloth and place under weights for 10-12 hours.

PASSE-PARTOUT

Using Cloth Tape

Passe-partout (Chapter XII) continues as a useful method for framing pictures for reasons which the writer finds valid. Artists in particular find this an inexpensive way to present their prints, drawings, or water colors. The use of colored mats with contrasting tape colors make this method a pleasing, space-saving way to show their work.

It is important that the framer keep in mind that the use of cellophane, masking or pressure-sensitive paper or cloth tape is not recommended for any but the most temporary work as the weight of the glass will frequently cause the assembly to slide apart.

GUMMED CLOTH TAPE (sometimes called bookbinders tape) comes in large rolls of black, white, brown, gray, etc., and is highly recommended. The 1" width is adequate for most jobs.

The following *is* suggested as a method for achieving a straight edge and an even amount of tape on the face of the glass. Use two 1" spring clamps to hold the picture and backing together and let it extend over the edge of the worktable. Place a weight on the glass so that the assembly doesn't shift. Now take a straight-edge—A ruler or piece of cardboard will do—and place it ¼" from the edge of the glass. It can be held in position with pieces of masking tape.

When applying the moistened tape, butt it against the straightedge and follow the procedure as described on pages 116-117.

While a cloth or sponge can be used for moisten-ing, a 2" brush dipped in water will be found more effective. Lay the tape with the *gummed side down* and wet the face side of the tape. Turn it over and wet the gummed side thoroughly. The glue on the tape is heavy so one does not need to hurry in applying it to the glass. Use a clean cloth for pressing it down.

Hangers

A note here about hangers may be of value. It will be necessary to attach the hangers before the picture is assembled and taped. A mirror hanger with a 1" brass paper fastener may be employed, or a hanger can be improvised which will be exceptionally secure, having a pull of over 25 pounds. This is assembled as follows: Cut a piece of metal strapping or other thin metal having smooth edges (about ½" wide) to a length of 2½". Bend it in half and bore or punch a ⅛" hole ¼" from the end through the two thicknesses. Cut a ½" slit in the center of the backing 3" down from the top. Spread the mirror hanger or the metal strip open

147

 and insert one-half in the slit. Slip a drapery ring under the strip, punch a hole through the backing, insert the paper fastener and spread it open on the other side. Tap the fastener flat with a hammer.

ASSEMBLING

An *Inexpensive Glass* Cleaner

Mix equal parts of denatured alcohol and water and a small quantity (1 to 2 ounces to a pint) of acetic acid or vinegar. Sprinkle on the glass, using one cloth for cleaning and another for wiping.

Gummed Kraft Tape for Sealing

A simple and effective way of sealing the backs of pictures after assembling is achieved with the use of GUMMED KRAFT TAPE, the most frequently useful width being 2". Stationery stores or industrial paper supply houses carry this item.

Cut four strips one inch or so longer than each side. Spread white or other glue on the back of the frame molding. Moisten the gummed side with a very wet cloth, attach the tape neatly and press down with a clean, damp cloth. Trim off the surplus end with a razor.

Gummed paper tape will always adhere properly to the backing and frame if this method is applied conscientiously.

EXPERIMENTAL FRAMES

Tipping on Pictures

Sometimes a very old print or a picture with irregular edges is enhanced when "tipped" on a mat covered with a special material and allowed to hang free, not pressed against the glass. For this presentation make a shadow-box frame and assemble it as described for pastels (page 76). The strip used to separate the picture from the glass can be of any thickness, depending on the effect desired.

Use gummed paper hinges or spots of glue or paste to attach the picture to the mat.

Covered *Inserts*

Original effects can be produced by covering the molding or insert, before assembling, with decoratively patterned or marbleized paper. This is then sized and coated with clear lacquer or shellac.

For instance, a narrow, light colored insert might be used surrounded by a much wider, flat frame covered with the decorative paper and the whole framed with a simple, medium-width, neutral finished frame.

CHAPTER SEVENTEEN

SOURCES *OF SUPPLIES*

SINCE LARGE QUANTITIES of materials are not generally needed in picture framing work, except for a few highly specialized items, all supplies can be purchased economically in retail stores. For this reason, only general classifications have been made. Some materials are sold under various trade names but are often made by the same manufacturer; it is difficult to detect any difference among them except price. If the retail stores in your locality do not handle a particular item, write to supply houses in large cities. It is also suggested that one refer to classified sections of telephone directories.

ADHESIVES:

Ground glue Rabbit
skin glue Synthetic
resin glue White glue
Source: Artists supply, hardware and paint
stores
Synthetic latex
Source: Wholesale adhesive manufacturers

FITTING AND HAND TOOLS:

Source: Hardware stores

Sources of Supplies

GLASS:
        Source: Hardware stores or wholesale glass
                dealers

MAT AND MOUNTING BOARD:
        Source: Artists supply stores or wholesale
                cardboard dealers

MAT KNIVES:
        Source: Artists supply or hardware stores

MITER VISES AND COMBINATION
  MITER VISE AND SAW:
        Source: Hardware stores or mail order houses

MOLDINGS:
  Builders finish
        Source: Lumber dealers
  Picture frame
        Source: See classified telephone directory
                or write to Chamber of Commerce
                of nearest city

PAINTING AND FINISHING MATERIALS:
        Source: Artists supply, hardware or paint
                stores

POINT-SETTER:
        Source: Hardware stores

POWER TOOLS:
        Source: Hardware stores or mail order houses

REPAIR STICKS:
        Source: Paint stores

ROLLERS AND STRAIGHTEDGES:
        Source: Hardware stores

INDEX

INDEX

153

INDEX

CPSIA information can be obtained at www.ICGtesting.com
Printed in the USA
OW07s1018140414

0596BV00006B/274/P

9 781438 288291